The Craig Charles
Almanac
of Total Knowledge

Craig Charles and Russell Bell

BOXTREE

For my dad, Joe; my son, Jack;
my rock, Suzanne, and the friends of Bill W.

Craig Charles

To Richard and Gaby Bell without whom
Russell Bell would not have been possible.

Russell Bell

First published in Great Britain in 1993 by Boxtree Limited,
Broadwall House, 21 Broadwall, London SE1 9PL

10 9 8 7 6 5 4 3 2 1

ISBN 1 85283 356 4

Designed and reproduced by Blackjacks, London
Photography by Paul Forrester
Illustrations by Arkadia
Photo retouching by Rupert at Scanners, 081-579 3193

Printed and bound in Great Britain

A CIP catalogue entry for this book is available from the British Library

Introduction

Well, here it is: a book. You don't realise how many pages there are in a book until you write one or until the school bully makes you eat an encyclopaedia page by page. When those terribly nice people at Boxtree asked me to write a book my first thought was, "Why?" closely followed by, "How?" and then, "What do I know about?" Well, I seem to have built a career out of talking very fast about endless different subjects and I seem to have got away with it. So, I

thought, I may as well write about that. Then I just had
to work out what to call it. Yes, I know what you're thinking:

The Craig Charles Almanac of Total Knowledge,

there's a modest little title, but as the great comedian and
mass murderer Vlad the Impaler once said: "If something's
worth doing, it's worth doing to excess," and he should
know. There, you see, history didn't record Vlad's phenome-
nal success as a comedian, you read it here first, but let me
assure you, if he cracked a joke, everyone for sixty square
miles creased up in hysterics. It is little snippets like this, as
well as little snippets like something else, that I shall be
including in this book.

All the facts in this book have been carefully researched
and collated. The results have been meticulously cross-refer-
enced and double checked, then stuck in a blender and
discarded. At best, leaving us with an interesting slant on
things and at worst, enough paper mache to make a passable
Trabant. Basically, this book is designed to give you a front
line defence against "The Experts" of this World. Those
people who narrow their specialist horizons to such an extent
that they learn more and more about less and less until finally
they know absolutely everything about nothing.

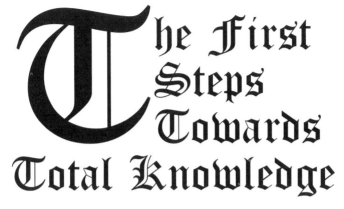

The First Steps Towards Total Knowledge

Prepare yourselves! We are about to embark upon our quest for total knowledge. For some of the more technical sections I consulted my old friend and colleague Professor Brain. Russell and I met the Professor at University College Toxteth where we were both studying the girls' gym class. We became such good friends that he allowed us to call him Dick and on many occasions the Professor would demonstrate his encyclopedic knowledge of almost everything whilst attempting to shake his dog, Sirius, off his leg. These brief but concise guides are the result of us pooling our knowledge, combining our resources and then asking someone who knew what the Hell they were talking about. However, much of the scientific wisdom in this chapter resulted from our many and varied conversations on a plethora of topics that often lasted well beyond the time when we were all asleep.

Now, the sum total of man's knowledge is increasing at such a rate that it is clearly impossible for any one person to know everything. However, this doesn't prevent certain individuals from trying to give the impression that not only do they know everything but also have a handle on a few things no one else has thought of.

The main ammunition in the battle to demonstrate total knowledge is 'Buzz Words'. Every specialist subject has its own vocabulary. 'Experts' always prefer to discuss their subject in this technical gobbledygook. This is because if they used normal language, people might realise that they don't really know what they're talking about.

A computer expert wouldn't say he was unhappy because his computer was running too slow so he modified it to work faster. He would say it was benchmarking at well under 25 megahertz so he installed a maths co-processor and a turbo retrofit to the front-end boot-up software.

You might think a floppy disc is a record that doesn't make it into the charts. Oh no, in the logic of computer-speak a floppy disc is a hard square thing.

By excluding people from a conversation like this you establish your mastery of a given subject as well as your credentials as bore of the year to anyone that doesn't speak your particular brand of nonsense. The people that do speak it will of course find you endlessly fascinating and try to outdo you with their knowledge of the latest 'Buzz Words' that they picked up from the last edition of *Numbers on the Back of Computers Weekly*.

There is, however, a way to beat them at their own game and that is to SOUND like you know what you're talking about. This will often panic them into changing the subject in case it transpires that you know more nonsense than them. The following chapter should enable you to waffle to a fairly high standard in a wide range of subjects including: Nuclear physics; Psychology; Philosophy; Biology; Metaphysics; Cosmology; Wine tasting and, of course, Country Lore.

A brief warning is in order at this point however: if the conversation looks like persisting beyond the realms of your two or three words of expert knowledge, change the subject by the simple expedient of saying "Look, this is all very interesting but I'm sure we're boring everyone else to death with all this technical jargon." Then proceed to introduce another -ology or two until you find one that nobody knows anything about. Then you can make up anything you want, no matter how fanciful, and everyone will think how incredibly clever you are and also how mind-numbingly boring. This is one of the many pitfalls of Total Knowledge and also the reason that most of this book is concerned, (hopefully), with humour: if you don't throw in a few gags, the eyes glaze over. People don't go out for a drink with their friends to be educated. They spent years trying to avoid that at school. They shouldn't be required to try to avoid it in their own time.

This chapter is not, as you may discover, the

ultimate guide to everything.

Someone far cleverer than me once said that anyone with a decent amount of common sense can learn 90% of the skills and knowledge required to do any job in the World in six

weeks. Clearly the remaining 10% is the bit that makes the difference between someone that is seriously good at his job and someone that is average and also doesn't take into consideration natural talent as in sports and art. But facts and tricks of the trade can be picked up very quickly. I once knew a chap who was out of work, then the next time I saw him he was obviously in the money. It transpired that his

best friend was a

deep sea diver for the North Sea oil rigs and had taught him the job in his front room and he was now, with the help of some photocopied certificates and his friend's close supervision, working in this highly specialised field and making a fortune.

I'm not for one second advocating that you should toddle off with a set of forged credentials and get a job as a brain surgeon, but it does show you what you can do if you put your mind to it. Hence this section of the book is designed to give you something to say about the subjects therein at any gathering of two or more people. Much of it might appear to be complete nonsense, but I'm confident you'll find the odd section which is pure rubbish.

Motor Racing

his is a sport played by a number of teams consisting of four people in overalls. For some reason the whole thing starts off with a lot of very fast cars spinning their back wheels and then organizing themselves into an orderly traffic jam at about two hundred miles per hour. This goes on for an hour or so.

While they are doing this a commentator discusses the merits of different types of tyres and the benefits of various forms of rubber until the race proper begins. This happens when one driver suddenly decides to change his tyres and drives into the pits, which are named after the bizarre subculture most motor sport enthusiasts inhabit. Then, the team have to change the car's tyres as quickly as possible. The team that changes the tyres in the shortest time wins the race. Then, for some reason they give the first driver over the line a bottle of champagne and pay him twenty million pounds. The one thing I can't work out is: why don't they use a decent set of tyres at the start of the bloody race? And another thing . . . why do they get paid twenty million pounds to drive like a nutter and I just get fined?

Well, that's motor racing for you. If you watch it regularly on TV it might be a good idea to seek professional help. This also applies to snooker, darts and unicycle hockey.

Country Lore

The country is that big green thing outside the cities that most of us live in. You can't miss it. It's full of trees and big animals and it smells sort of "natural". There are many things the city dweller should know before venturing into this verdant hinterland but first a warning: there are many strange things in the country that you won't have come across in the city. Now, we all know what a chicken looks like, right? Well, in the country they have chickens with heads on that run around on little legs and aren't even frozen. They have other animals that are bigger than people, for God's sake. You know those knobbly things you make chips out of? They dig them out of the ground in the country.

There should really be a large sign outside the country saying "Here there be dragons" because if you don't know what you're doing you may never be seen again. Take a friend of mine. He neglected to close the gate to a field and a massive, ruddy faced humanoid spliced his gruttocks and mullioned every thrussock he had. He wasn't a pretty sight after that.

In fact he was an ugly site, (sic) as opposed to a beauty spot which is something they have in the country. A beauty spot looks exactly the same as the rest of the countryside except it's full of people going, "Ooh, isn't it lovely," which it probably would be if it wasn't full of people going, "Ooh, isn't it lovely." This is one of the many paradoxes associated with "The Country" and one of the reasons why it might be a good place to avoid. Unless of course "Daddy owns it", then you can invite your friends down to sit on some of the big animals. There are many strange jobs on offer in the country. I once met a chap whose job it was to stick the chicken crap and feathers onto free-range eggs so you knew they were the real thing. "Nice work if you can get it," I hear you say but if you could see the shoes required you might have second thoughts. In the country "stile" is something you walk over, not something you have.

There are very few shops in the country, but the ever resourceful farm folk have come up with a number of ingenious, if disgusting, ploys to circumvent this inconvenience.

They can't just go out and buy a box of milk like proper people, so what do they do? THEY SQUEEZE IT OUT OF A COW! God only knows who first came up with that one, but it seems to work. Apparently cows are full of the stuff.

I could go on about what they do with manure, I could tell you the awful truth about sausages, but you wouldn't believe me, and if you did you'd probably never eat again so I'll leave it here. I hope now that you have a better understanding of what awaits you if you should be foolish enough to turn off the motor-way.

Quotes   *I don't mind sleeping on an empty stomach provided it isn't my own. (Philip J.Simborg)*

Words

Most sentences start to look pretty insubstantial if you take all the words out. In fact you're just left with a line of punctuation which can be almost as boring as some daytime TV shows. So, words are obviously very important on the writing and conversation front. All I'm going to put in this section is a list of fifty happening words that will make anyone sound extremely intelligent, especially if you use them in the right context. If English is a rich language, these words are the triple chocolate layer cake with double cream of linguistics but don't use too many or, like the cake, you'll make people sick.

Anomaly an irregularity of behaviour or motion.

Abscond to secretly leg it.

Abstruse difficult to understand.

Amalgam mixture or blend.

Bowdlerize to censor.

Bumptious conceited or pushy.

Choleric hot tempered.

Coalesce to fuse or merge.

Demographic relating to births, deaths and characteristics of the populace.

Didactic something that teaches or instructs.

Dolorous sad; painful.

Evanescent fading quickly; almost imperceptible.

Phlegmatic unemotional; sluggish.

Hedonist one who is devoted to pleasure.

Hyperbole exaggerated statement.

Internecine mutually destructive.

Insensate unfeeling; without sensation.
Judicious wise; sensible.
Lambaste to criticise severely.
Libertine someone without moral restraints.
Loquacious talkative or wordy.
Malediction a curse.
Cachet prestige; status symbol.
Coterie an exclusive group.
Cursory hasty; without attention to detail.
Sedentary describing someone who sits down a lot.
Scintillating sparkling, either literally or figuratively.
Tautology unnecessary repetition of words or ideas.
Tautology unnecessary repetition of words or ideas
Obloquy verbal abuse; violent, insulting speech.
Peripatetic moving from place to place.
Progenitor ancestor of person, animal or plant.
Recherche extremely rare.
Rueful regretful.
Voracious having an insatiable appetite.

Votary dedicated follower.
Vacuous empty; unintelligent; expressionless.
Verdant covered with green plants.
Arcane mysterious.
Germane relevant to the topic under discussion.
Antithesis exact opposite of something.
Brackish unpleasant tasting.
Prosaic dull.
Plethora an excess of.
Rapscallion a rogue.
Toothsome delicious to eat.
Ubiquitous seen everywhere.
Persiflage repartee.

I must reiterate that these heavy calibre words should be used very sparingly. However, if you are still at school, see if your teacher can put together a paragraph or two containing all the above words (don't let them see the definitions). That'll get them sweating. Very few people know what "internecine" means let alone "obloquy."

Many an interesting insight lies hidden within certain names and phrases. I find it amazing that

Quotes   *In spite of the cost of living, it's still popular. (Kathleen Norris)*

SCHOOLMASTER is an anagram of THE CLASS-ROOM and that the only anagram of MONDAY is DYNAMO but then, I'm funny like that. For your amusement I offer some interesting anagrams of well known names and institutions, starting with what must be the most amazing anagram in history.

VIRGINIA BOTTOMLEY
  I'm an evil tory bigot
GREAT BRITAIN
  Trite bargain
UNITED STATES OF AMERICA
  Customised fattie arena
AUSTRALIANS
  Ass at urinal
UNITED GERMANY
  Enraged mutiny
THE ENGLAND TEAM
  Hated gentleman
LIVERPOOL FC
  Cop overfill
THE MIDDLE EAST
  Them deadliest
PARLIAMENT
  Rampant lie Partial men
  Armpit lane Ale in tramp
  Anal permit
THE LABOUR PARTY
  O brutal therapy

RUPERT MURDOCH
  Retouch Dr. Rump
NORMAN LAMONT
  Not normal man
MICHAEL HESELTINE
  Hellish tie menace
  Alien heel chemist
ROBBIE COLTRANE
  Recreation blob
  O terrible bacon
THE GREEN PARTY
  The energy trap
NOEL EDMONDS
  Mended loons
  Sodden lemon
BOB MONKHOUSE
  Bum honks oboe
RONALD REAGAN
  Arranged loan
SADDAM HUSSEIN
  Mad anus hissed
  Amid sunshades
  A sad Hindu mess
PRESIDENT CLINTON
  Nondescript inlet

{While he's not looking, here are some anagrams of **CRAIG CHARLES**, R.B.}

Clear rich gas; He is Carl Crag; Clair charges; Scare rich gal; Ace girls arch; Large rich sac; Chair legs care; His car, leg car; Garlic arches; Glacier crash; Eric shag Carl

Quotes *Some condoms are made of sheep's intestines, but I was so scared the first time I wore the whole sheep.*
(Danny Williams)

Advertising

Advertising is the art of conveying the maximum amount of impressive nonsense in the minimum number of words. Its ultimate aim is to create within you the idea that your life will be meaningless and unfulfilled unless you drive a certain four wheeled box, wearing clothes that have been washed in a certain kind of gunk with a particular bar of brown sweet stuff sticking out of your face. But then that's glamour for you.

This is achieved by paying people who don't look like the rest of the Human race (See SUPER MODELS) to pretend that they drive six thousand pound cars, eat tons of chocolate and wear reasonably priced clothes. I fall for it every time. There is another little trick the ad men are always using: they will state that one product is special because it uses ingredient "X".

The fact that every other similar product uses the same ingredient is irrelevant, they don't mention it. Here are a few examples:

"I like BLIMPY bread because

they use REAL yeast in the baking." So does everybody else, but because they bother to mention it the implication is that everyone else is using sawdust or something.

"Bumflap car tyres are made of REAL rubber."

"You won't find any cyanide in Clutterbucks chocolates."

"Rumdoo food mixers, the ones that WON'T rip your face off."

"There's no plankton in SO-SO petrol."

"Cloggy Corn Flakes. No dead fish in the box or your money back."

This is what the ad men call a U.S.P. which is a unique selling proposition. However, as the vast majority of products are incredibly ordinary they have to invent one: "Hobbelsteins beer, specially brewed so it DOESN'T dissolve your internal organs". As if all this wasn't enough, there is one more insidious weapon in the marketing arsenal: THE JINGLE. The jingle is a musical maggot that worms it's way into your brain and sits there singing at you. If,

God forbid, we are ever involved in another war we don't need an army. All we have to do is send over a marvellous character called Jonathan Hodge to write jingles at the enemy. Remember "Do the shake and vac and put the freshness back . . ."? That was one of his. They'll be on their knees in no time.

Quotes
Blondes have more fun because they're easier to find in the dark.

Self Motivation

There is a wonderful device you can construct very easily to promote self motivation: take a piece of string and tie a loop in one end. Pass the loop over your right foot until it is round your ankle. Then pass the string over the back of your right shoulder and give it a sharp pull, thus kicking yourself up the bum.

Survivalism

Over the years I have picked up a number of useful tips on surviving in different environments. After many hours in the field I have distilled two cardinal rules to which the seminal survivalist should always adhere:

i)   Wrap up warm.

ii) Take plenty of food.

Also, if you are going to be in a particularly hostile environment, a machine gun could be useful. Now, there is always the possibility that you could run out of food. Never fear. In this situation you can resort to an old "Hunter gatherer" technique known as "Ordering a takeaway". Of course if you find yourself in a remote spot with a very poor choice of takeaway restaurants you may have to resort to the "Checking into a hotel and calling room service" ploy, but this can prove unreliable and several S.A.S. men have been known to have died of starvation waiting for a geriatric night porter to arrive with a plate of ham and cheese sandwiches "'Cos that's all there is left in the kitchen don't you know it's after midnight I'll be up as soon as I can but you know I'll have to make them myself and with my legs and all."

For surviving on the Moors I can't stress enough the importance of a good tourist guide and a reliable air conditioned caravan with a microwave oven, shower and well stocked fridge-freezer. Then, if you should come across some poor unfortunate, huddled in a makeshift lean-to, trying to start a fire with a piece of flint and a survival knife so he can cook a smelly pot of moss and earthworms you can invite him in, brew up the Earl Grey and without being too smug, point out the benefits of proper survival training while you cook him a nice plate of chicken fricassee.

In harsh or extreme circumstances such as a plane crash in the Andes you may have to resort to unusual and extreme measures to survive. I know it may sound disgusting in the cosy confines of civilisation, but it may be necessary for you to resort to actually eating the airline food, unless of course there are any other passengers left that you haven't already eaten.

In desert conditions, there is one very important survival technique to remember: take loads and loads of water with you. It gets hot as Hell out there and this will make you thirstier than a whole packet of pork scratchings. It's incredible how many people die of thirst in deserts every year just because they didn't take plenty of water. Well, there you go. The ultimate guide to survival. So don't come snivelling to me with a nasty chill because you forgot to pack your caravan. Remember, once you turn off the main road, you're on your own out there.

Antiques

Generally speaking antiques are things that used to be everyday items when they were made, but are now worth fortunes because there are so few left, which either means they were badly made in the first place or so unpopular at the time that they didn't make very many.

As a general rule if something is old and superbly made it will be valuable. If it is old and crap it will very likely fall into the category that experts refer to as "Old crap". Occasionally some "Old crap" is valuable because it was so crappily made that only two specimens managed to survive the ravages of time. Invariably, it will turn out that the Queen has one in the back of a drawer at Buck House and someone called Arthur will discover the other in an attic in Swindon. This is why the antiques game is so dodgy, unless of course your name is Arthur and you live in Swindon.

One of the most exciting things to do in the World of antiques is to try and guess what present day piece of junk will be worth a fortune in times to come. In general, if, tomorrow, you buy a superbly made item from a well known craftsman for an arm and a leg, in two hundred years it will be worth an arm, two legs, four lungs, six kidneys and a spleen. They might even throw in a pancreas if you haggle.

Professor Brain Explains

part 1

PHYSICS

ALBERT EINSTEIN said the faster you go the heavier you get and the longer you live. This applies to everything except racing drivers. He also said E=MC2 and no one at the time was bright enough to argue. There is only one physicist worth worrying about at the moment and that is Dr STEPHEN HAWKING. His book *A Brief History of Time* is a classic of the genre. Virtually everyone with intellectual pretensions and a coffee table bought it.

However, no-one could understand it, so physics is a marvellous arena in which to talk a load of old nonsense. I'm personally writing a book along similar lines entitled *A Timely History of Briefs* in which I postulate a hitherto unknown relationship between the Y front and the boxer short. But I digress. Here are a few good things to throw into any conversation on physics or cosmology.

THE BIG BANG

The 'Big Bang Theory' is clearly drivel. Forget all those multi-dimensional energy interchanges, neutronium eggs and singularities that expand into a sort of 'Inflatable Instant Universe Kit'. None of this works for one simple reason: IN SPACE NO ONE CAN HEAR YOU SCREAM let alone go bang, so that one's an obvious non-starter.

The only thing I know that was ever created by a bloody great explosion is a bloody great hole. Q.E.D. (In science it is always good to say Q.E.D. after anything you are not sure about. It stands for *Quod Erat Demonstrandum*, which is Latin for "So don't argue with ME you bastard.")

RELATIVITY

This is a relatively simple concept as well and has already been lightly touched upon, if not lovingly caressed, in the Einstein section. If you fly round the moon and back in a spaceship travelling at very close to the speed of light, you will arrive back in time to see yourself taking off. If you do this eleven times there will be enough of you to have a game of five-a-side football with yourself AND have an impartial referee.

If you get lost in any conversation about physics merely pipe up with: "But what about Heisenberg's Uncertainty Principle?" This basically states that you can never know where the Hell anything is, how fast it's going or what it had for lunch. It usually shuts most people up.

TIME

TIME is a concept invented by Man. Probably a Swiss man come to think of it. Man required a vocabulary to describe the order of events in his life, so he invented the watch. Then he put a picture of Mickey Mouse on it. But then that's progress for you.

Should some smart-arse begin discussing his pet theories about TIME, ask him this one: "If a stopped clock is right twice a day, how many times a day is a perfectly functioning clock right?"

This should keep him baffled long enough for you to chat up his girl-friend.

There are many anomalies associated with time. If you invented a time machine that could go into the future a millisecond at a time, it would be just like living in the present. I was a little confused last week when someone asked me if I had any spare time. What is spare time? Is it like that little lever you pull on an aqualung to give you a few more minutes of air while you try to get your flipper out of a giant clam? If people really do have 'spare time', why do some of them spend it train spotting? Why don't friends say things like "Can you lend me a couple of hours until the weekend? I've got a whole afternoon you can have next Tuesday but there's this girl I'm seeing on Saturday . . ."

Why aren't there beggars in the street asking if you've got any spare time? It makes no sense to me at all. I haven't got any spare time. I need it all.

There should be enough material there for you to baffle anyone on the question of TIME.

SUB ATOMIC PARTICLES

The intellectuals among you will have read my definitive book on this subject already. For those of you who have yet to read *Everything's Made Of Really Little Bits*, I shall treat you to a brief summary. One of the most important quests for any physicist is to discover the basic building block of all matter. Whatever this particle turns out to be, one thing is for sure: it's going to be seriously small.

Most physicists agree that there are six really small bits when it comes to sub-atomic particles but they can't have been in a very steady state when they named them.

I mean, who in their right mind would spend years finding the damned things and then call them; up, down, charmed, strange, bottom and top. Imagine being a sub-atomic particle. You wait millennia to be discovered and then some boffin goes and calls you Bottom. Nice.

However, fear not, for I have discovered some particles that make all the above look like footballs, on the atomic scale of things. Here are just a few.

Quotes *You can judge the character of a man by how he treats those who can do nothing for him or to him.*

Tackyons   Cheap nasty little particles that are better forgotten.

Baccyons   Small particles that fall out of badly made roll-ups.

Cantons   Very tasty little particles that you can order by 'phone.

Inventorrs   Particles that cheating physicists make up to balance a tricky equation. (See gluons).

Gluons   Particle track that cheating physicists glue onto a bubble chamber photograph to make it look as if something new is happening. (See inventorrs).

Marks & Sensors   Good value particles that return to where they came from if they don't fit a given equation.

Hardons   Large particles that exhibit a complete lack of conscience.

Zircons   Look like real sub-atomic particles but on closer inspection are completely bogus and worthless.

Suckons   The most attractive particles in the Universe. Gravity is entirely due to the action of these little suckers.

Wheezons   Slow moving particles that seem to have trouble catching their breath.

Bonbons   Sweet little particles with a light dusting of sugar.

Dadooronrons   Good time particles that move in an erratic, jiving sort of path.

Quotes   *Every time I look at you I get a fierce desire to be lonesome. (Oscar Levant)*

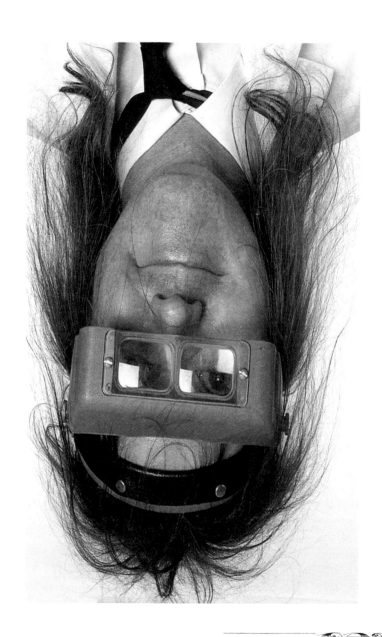

Quotes A person may be worth a million pounds and still be worthless.

SPACE

Contrary to popular belief, Space is not huge. It's just somewhere to be huge in. In a list of substantial things, however, Space is right at the bottom, just under 'Nothing'. If you took all the Space in the Universe and put it in a milk bottle, all you would have is a milk bottle, albeit an incredibly empty one.

Although it's not there, Space is affected by gravitational fields. In the presence of a large mass, Space becomes dented. A bit like a fat lady sitting on a bed. This is why the path of a beam of light bends as it passes a star and hence why you can never see Pavorotti properly at any of his concerts.

Nature abhors a vacuum almost as much as it hates tourists, which is strange because Nature contrived to make it the main component of the universe. Now, life and vacuums don't mix, and I don't just mean socially. We're talking boiling blood and eyes popping out here. Vacuums do have their uses here on Earth though. You can keep tea hot for one thing. However, there are more sinister uses: Archie 'The Pucker' Sarducci, the infamous Mafia hit-man, used to shut his victims in a wardrobe and suck all the air out through a straw. And if you believe that, feel free to send me all your valuables, care of the publishers.

Quotes   Q: *How horny can you get?*
A: *I don't know, what's the record?*
(*Neil Simon*)

Stunning Facts to Boggle the Mind

There are few things to rival the satisfaction of seeing incredulity on the face of someone to whom you have just imparted an amazing fact. A lull in any conversation can be bridged by one or two of these snippets of little-known information but avoid too many. There is nothing in this World more boring than a long stream of "Interesting Facts". Also, all such anecdotes should be prefaced by the words, "Did you know," in a Michael Caine accent in deference to the man who actually invented interesting facts.

1

Before tea or coffee were introduced into Britain the normal, everyday beverage was beer. In the seventeenth century, nurses in hospitals would receive an allowance of two pints per day and children were allocated two gallons a week each. Maybe this is where the phrase "The good old days" originated.

2

In the harem of Chief Akkiri, ruler of the Estuary of Calabar, Nigeria, a girl called Mum-Zi became pregnant shortly after her betrothal. Not very unusual except that the girl was seven at the time. Amazingly the daughter she gave birth to also became pregnant and gave birth at the age of eight, making Mum-Zi the youngest grandmother on record at the age of seventeen.

3

Some people often over-react in a given situation but Mohammed II, The Sultan of Turkey from 1451 to 1481 surely takes the biscuit. After being called away from the dinner table on some urgent matter, he returned to find his desert, a slice of melon, had disappeared. He was so angry he interrogated the fourteen Royal attendants present and when they all denied the theft he ordered the court physician to cut open the stomachs of the pages to find the guilty party. Not one of them contained any trace of the missing melon. Mohammed apologised and ordered another desert.

4

There have been some hard cases in history but a Greek chap called Theogenes is not someone whose drink you'd

have wanted to knock over. A native of Thasos, Theogenes served a cruel prince named Thesus and competed as a gladiator around 900 BC.
One popular 'game' at the time involved two men being strapped, sitting, onto two large flat stones, toe to toe, and then hitting each other with their fists, which were wrapped in leather strips with metal spikes, until one fell over dead. During his career Theogenes faced 1,425 men . . . and killed them all. Hard or what?

5

Lemmings, as we all know, are not renowned for their survival abilities. However, when a lemming burrow was excavated in 1967 the remains were found to be 10,000 years old. Now, although the lemmings were long dead, seeds of an Arctic tundra shrub, Lupinus Articus, were found. These were carefully planted by scientists and germinated within 48 hours. I can't even grow fresh cress.

Continued on page 124

Quotes   *You'll never meet anyone who doesn't think their cat should be in a commercial.*

Entertaining Members of the Yakuza in Your Home

The YAKUZA are the Japanese equivalent of the Mafia. They are usually heavily tattooed and have a tendency towards seriousness. However, this doesn't detract from the fact that they can make very pleasant houseguests if you follow one or two simple rules.

i) If a member of the YAKUZA asks for anything at all, including your wife, it is customary to give it to him. As he enters your home it is traditional to inform him that he should consider everything in your house to be his. Should you be fortunate enough to be invited to his house, he will, in his turn, let you know that everything in his house is also his.

ii) Do not look at, talk to or grin at a member of the YAKUZA unless he is holding you against the wall by your throat. In this case it is considered allowable, and in some cases desirable, for you to gurgle.

iii) If a member of the YAKUZA fails in any task he will indicate his apologetic state of mind by cutting off one of his fingers. To be prepared for this eventuality, you should always have a sharp knife handy as well as a chopping board and a box of elastoplast. Electric carving knives are considered vulgar for this application. This practice is at the root of the only known Yakuza joke. If you want to reduce your guest to helpless laughter merely waggle your fingers in front of his face saying, "I've got more than you-hoo" in a singsong voice.

iv) It is considered good manners to anticipate the desires of your guest and to this end it is usually wise to give him all your money as he comes through the door and then to begin loading any valuables you may have into the back of his car.

v) In return for your hospitality it is usual for your guest to invite you to stand in a bath full of water while he throws in the ceremonial electric fire. It is considered bad manners to refuse this invitation.

vi) Many YAKUZA carry a Katana, or what we in the West might refer to as a "sodding great three foot razor". If you are particularly fortunate your YAKUZA guest might demonstrate the keen edge of his Katana by cutting you into fifteen or sixteen pieces, but still keep you alive. This charming and ancient custom dates back to the time when the Japanese used to like cutting people into fifteen or sixteen pieces.

vii) If a member of the YAKUZA sticks a short knife into you, remember, it is just his way of saying "I felt like sticking a short knife into you". In this circumstance, it is considered bad manners to scream or to bleed on any of your guest's garments.

viii) At the end of the day, a member of the YAKUZA will be a friend for life unless you look at him, address him directly, mention his name in company, allow your shadow to fall across any of his belongings or go near him. If these simple rules are followed you will find the YAKUZA to be the most charming of house guests.

the **P**aranormal

(and Yachting)

THE PARANORMAL

Much of the Paranormal is associated with what the experts call E.S.P. This stands for Extremely Strange People. These people have the ability to know of events before they happen, the ability to know what other people are thinking and the ability to move objects without any obvious contact. These are called respectively: clairvoyance, telepathy and stealing.

I once experienced a strange phenomenon in a room full of people when we all had exactly the same thought at exactly the same time. Outside the window there was a tremendous crash, an explosion and a cry of "Save the iguana". At that precise moment, every single person in that room thought "What the bloody Hell was that all about?" Uncanny as that may be, it pales into insignificance when compared to another experience I had in Stoke Poges. I saw a wallet on the pavement and picked it up. Suddenly, I had a strange impulse and, following it, I held the wallet up to my face and concentrated fiercely. In less than five minutes I knew the name of the owner and exactly where he lived. Some people put this down to the fact that his name and address were written on the wallet, but I see it as a definite paranormal experience.

It has been demonstrated that you can sharpen a razor by placing it in a pyramid. If you bear in mind that a pyramid would cost about four billion pounds to build at today's prices and would also take about twenty years to finish, then I think you'll agree that the smart money is on buying a packet of disposable safety razors for seventy five pee.

YACHTING

I'm sure yachting is a marvellous sport, but I've found you can get the same effect by sitting in front of a fan and getting a friend to throw buckets of cold water over you every couple of seconds whilst hitting you over the head with a lump of wood, yelling, "Jibe ho" and flapping a bed sheet in your face.

Quotes *The only way to have a friend is to be one (Ralph Waldo Emerson)*

the Music Business

All I can say about the music business is that unless you're one of those weirdos that likes the idea of vast amounts of money, fame, adulation and gorgeous members of the opposite sex throwing themselves on you shouting "Take me, take me" then stay well clear of it.

Meeting Royalty

A GUIDE TO MODERN ETIQUETTE

1 If a member of the Royal family offers their hand for you to shake, it is considered bad form to whip your hand away at the last moment, place your thumb on your nose and waggle your fingers.

2 It is considered less than courteous to blow a raspberry when a member of the Royal Family bends over. Unless they've done it to you first.

3 It is usually frowned upon to nick things when the butler isn't looking.

4 One shouldn't grab a member of the Royal family and say, "Gotcha" unless they have "Gotcha'd" you first.

5 When shaking hands, the Royal family generally wear white gloves. This is not protocol, it's because they don't like touching scum. If you want to amuse a member of the Royal family, shake hands with one of them then look at your hand, put your tongue out, go 'Urgh' and rub your hand on your jacket. This always cracks them up.

6 If a corgi starts humping your leg it is permissable to make one attempt to stun it with a blunt object. If this fails you should leave the creature to it. Try to be flattered. If the Queen is watching, fake an orgasm. The Queen likes corgi lovers.

7 If you feel an irresistible urge to break wind at the dinner table, call over a member of the serving staff, let rip and blame it on them.

8 It is considered bad form to ask if you can 'crash out' for a few hours after a Royal banquet, unless of course you've brought your own sleeping bag.

9 Generally speaking, if you are invited to a Royal household, you shouldn't really turn up with a load of pissed mates.

10 At the dinner table, it is considered bad manners to ask if you can put the football on. Unless of course it's a cup match, in which case it will probably be on anyway.

11 Never grope a member of the Royal family unless you are invited to, or you think you can get away with it.

12 When arriving at Buckingham Palace one should not chain one's bike to the railings at the front. Instead, approach one of the guards, and ask if you can leave it in his little hut. These chaps are extremely hard and have guns, so you can rest assured they are well able to look after your bike.

Quotes *Won't you come into my garden? I would like my roses to see you. (Good romantic one. Richard Brinsley Sheridan "To a young Lady")*

Fashion

The recycling of old ideas in such a way as to make them look original. Fashion can largely be summed up by the shape of lapels, the cut of trousers and the length of skirts. The one constant in fashion seems to be that every decade it comes up with something that involves women wearing less than the decade before and charging twice as much as the previous year. By the end of the decade designers will be charging £100,000 to send you onto the streets naked with one of their labels stuck on your bum. Basically, at the end of the day it's the label you're paying for so it seems quite a logical progression to get rid of the clothes altogether.

War (and football)

ars are only ever started for two reasons: religion or greed. Usually both. A dictator will have a peek over the fence, notice a few acres of prime turnip fields and say, "Right, I'm having those and it's morally justifiable because everyone in that country worships Og who is a false god and we have the mighty Wumberdum on our side so we can't fail to triumph."

Sound familiar? But there's another great problem with war: it's so good for business. Much of the economy of many countries revolves around their defence budgets. Also, you must remember that every new weapon that the ingenious minds of the arms manufacturers dream up will sell better if it can be shown to kill vast numbers of people with very little effort. The only politically correct way to test these devices is to have a cosy little war, miles away from your own country and see what works the best. Remember Vietnam, Korea, the Falklands? The star of the Falklands wasn't a general, it was the French Exocet missile. In the Middle East, the Patriot missiles were top of the hit parade and I'm sure sales of these extremely anti-social devices went through the roof, as did half the missiles.

Wars are becoming a bit unfashionable, so it might not be a bad idea to make football a permanent substitute for war. You still have that sense of National identity and not quite so many people get hurt. Europe could put aside its petty nationalistic differences and form a European eleven. You could have Helmut Kohl in goal. Not because it rhymes, but because he's a fat bastard. Margaret Thatcher on the right wing, wearing a completely different strip to everybody else and telling everyone how to play. Norman Tebbit would be a useful player, there's no danger of hand ball when you're wearing a straight jacket. Le Pen could be a referee and send off anyone of dubious racial extraction. There would obviously be a Swedish physiotherapist ready with a bit of executive massage and the Norwegians could charge extortionate prices on the gate. Finally, of course, we could have four Belgians as corner flags and the Russians could queue up for the oranges at half time.

Quotes   *A woman is like a tea-bag: you never know her strength until she's in hot water. (Nancy Reagan)*

Modern Chat-Up Lines

These come in two sections:

a) The naff ones.
b) The really naff ones.

SECTION A

"Excuse me, but I've just come out of a Buddhist retreat after five years of contemplation and I wondered if you might know somewhere where I could stay for a few days while I sort out what to do with the LA mansion I just inherited from my spiritual master at the monastery."

"Hello, I've just arrived in town, have you noticed how many weirdos there are around here? Look, I know it might sound a little brash of me but . . . can I make soup out of your underwear?"

"My God, what a life. I've spent twelve years training to be a sexual therapist but am I happy? I'm sure a lot of people would be quite satisfied dishing out multiple orgasms to clients day in and day out, but I want more out of life. I mean, what's the point of being a multi-billionaire if you can't enjoy it?"

"Of course it's possible for men and women to be friends. It's also perfectly possible for men and women to sleep together without anything happening. Just come back to my place tonight and I'll prove it."

SECTION B

(For the less caring members of the community:)
"Do you wanna go halves on a baby?"

(For the politically correct potential partner:)
"How can you refuse a child life by not sleeping with me?"

(For the kinky, politically correct potential partner:)
"I want to take you home and rub your body all over with baby oil that hasn't been tested on animals."

(For the sick intellectual potential partner:)
"Will you take me home, tie me up and call me rude names in Latin?"

(If you're feeling a bit crawly)
"I don't have sex with women any more. I don't think it's necessary. I just like kissing and cuddling and being with someone."
I can't tell you how many times that one's got me laid.

Quotes   *If little Bo Peep lost her sheep today the EEC would pay her for not finding them. ("Observer" Sunday Times.)*

Wine

If anyone opens a bottle of wine and asks your opinion there are only three or four things you have to remember: Smell the cork. If it smells like vinegar the wine is probably "corked" which is a euphemism for crap. If it smells like wine, take a sip, smack your lips together and make a face like a fish. Then say "Not bad . . . perhaps a little long on the tongue." No-one knows what this means but only wine experts say it so it must convey something. Then, you should say "I think I prefer the 83." This is always a fairly safe bet as 83 was a good year for virtually every kind of wine in Europe. Most of the wines from that vintage are very good for "laying down". This means that if you drink more than two bottles you will almost certainly end up laying down. Of course, if the wine you are tasting is an 83, you will look like a complete wally.

The pictures on these pages demonstrate the consequences of over indulging in wine.

the P professions

LAW

Basically, all you have to do to be a professional in the law game is dress up in a black robe, put on a daft wig and argue. The gown and wig are traditional throwbacks to the time when people in the legal profession would moonlight as pantomime dames to make a few extra shillings.

There is only one set of rules you need to know when practising Law. If the facts are against you, argue the law. If the law is against you, argue the facts. If both are against you, call the other lawyer names.

ACCOUNTANCY

Accountants add up lots of small sums of money until they have one big number. They write this number in a book with a lot of other numbers. They also fill in lots of forms and help people to cheat the Government. There is nothing you can say about accountants that hasn't already been said about formica.

ARCHITECTURE

There is nothing about architecture you can't learn by playing with Meccano and Lego. If you want to start a brand new style of architecture just copy something old and call it Neo-Oldism. Ironically, the few radically original buildings that do occasionally get put up look as if they WERE designed using Meccano and Lego.

BUSINESS

There is only one rule you need to remember if you want to be a successful business person: buy something cheap and sell it for more money. This is the first and last rule of business and is all you need to know to make trillions of pounds, (But don't tell anyone.)

There is one other aspect of business that may be worth considering. Some people got bored with the Buy cheap; Sell Dear game so they invented SPECULATION. This consists of buying something that doesn't exist with money you don't have and selling it back to the people that didn't have it in the first place for more than you didn't pay for it, keeping the difference. Unbelievably, some people seem to make a lot of money doing this.

Another way to make a fortune is to invent something.
All you have to do is invent a better mouse trap. Then find loads of people with better mice they want to get rid of and you're in business. Who ever said making money was difficult?

Quotes   *There is nothing worse than a "Now" look with a "Then" face (Dave Falk)*

History

The problem with history is that as soon as you think you've learned it, you've got another day to catch up on. Man seems doomed to make history until he starts learning from it which, unfortunately, looks unlikely. Ancient History used to be a lot cheaper to make than it is now but, even at today's prices, we still churn it out.

I was intending to cover the entire history of the World in this chapter but it would have taken too long so I'm just going to stick to the last two thousand years. There's no point being too ambitious. Also, instead of mentioning everything that happened, which would take about two thousand years, I'm just going to deal with History century by century and pick out what, for me, were the seminal events of that era.

1ST CENTURY AD

Romans invade Britain in Latin. This disturbs the locals who were busy painting themselves blue and shouting a lot, pre-empting Chelsea supporters by two thousand years. Boudicca objected and gave them a right kicking.

2ND CENTURY AD

Times were hard and they couldn't afford to make any history for a while but things picked up around the 8th century.

3RD TO 7TH CENTURIES

Nothing happened.

8TH CENTURY AD

Ecgfrith became ruler of the Anglian Kingdom of Mercia. However, he lasted less than a year because no-one could pronounce his name. Also, the Omayyad Abederrahman founded the Caliphate of Cordoba and a state paper mill was set up in Baghdad. Whoever said history was boring?

9TH CENTURY AD

The Danes raided England and sacked London, raping, pillaging and forcing people to eat bacon with writing on. The Arabs sacked Marseille but settled in Southern Italy once they smelt the docks.

10TH CENTURY AD

Erik Bloodaxe is driven to give up a promising career in flower arranging due to cruel taunts about his somewhat uncompromising name. Deciding to live up to it, he begins methodically killing people until he is ruler of Norway.

Quotes *A gossip is one who talks to you about others; a bore is one who talks to you about himself, and a brilliant conversationalist is one who talks to you about yourself. (Lisa Kirk)*

11TH CENTURY AD

King Harold invented the monocle, shortly before dying at Hastings.

12TH CENTURY AD

Alfonso IX the Slobberer (that really was his name) became ruler of Leon. Urban III became Pope and gave his name to a Industrial House album. Henry the Proud loses Bavaria to Leopold but leaves Henry the Lion as his heir, the only glove puppet ever to rule Saxony.

13TH CENTURY AD

Walther von der Vogelweide, the greatest German poet of that name, sadly passed away. Boniface of Savoy became the first pedigree Archbishop of Canterbury. Superstitious people had a very bad time during this century.

14TH CENTURY AD

Nothing happened again.

15TH CENTURY AD

The Turks conquer Smyrna and take Constantinople, Salonika, and Athens although they had a row about the Acropolis. Then they conquered Serbia, Morea, Trebizond, Bosnia, Herzegovina, and Negroponte, spreading fear and kebabs throughout the region.

Quotes *It's so easy to have a fatal accident and ruin your life. (Tony Blackburn.)*

16TH CENTURY AD

Henry VIII became England's first royal serial killer.

17TH CENTURY AD

The Mayflower left Plymouth for Massachusetts to check out some likely sites for McDonalds restaurants. The first sign they put up said: "More than two sold."

18TH CENTURY AD

Josephine went down in history and made Napoleon's day.

19TH CENTURY AD

Pneumatic tyres and football. Sex was invented in 1843 and immediately banned.

20TH CENTURY AD

In an attempt to avoid the parking problems in New York, some Americans land on the Moon, England win the World Cup and **The Craig Charles Almanac of Total Knowledge** is published, changing the World of Literature as we know it.

Professor Brain Explains

part 2

PHILOSOPHY

Most philosophers try to answer the question "Why are we here?" I've always felt that the question "Why do they bother?" is more interesting but I suppose it keeps them off the streets so we may as well leave them to it. This is a good section to read last thing at night if you suffer from insomnia.

DESCARTES Once said "I think therefore I am" which surprised a lot of his friends who didn't speak English. Certain people suspect that this wasn't, in fact, his philosophy of life but a cryptic clue from a crossword he was stuck on.
JEAN-PAUL SARTRE was an existentialist. Here are a few quotes of his to toss

around: "When the rich wage war it's the poor who die." "I am condemned to be free." "Three o'clock is always too late or too early for anything you want to do." "I hate victims who respect their executioners." And the one that sums up a good deal of his philosophy: "My thought is me: that's why I can't stop. I exist by what I think... and I can't prevent myself from thinking." Basically he was trying to say "I think, therefore I am." However, I think one of the wisest things he ever said was: "Hell is being locked in a room for eternity with your friends" because, if you think about it, all his friends were French. Now, that was just a tiny little snippet of his life's work so, in order not to lose any more readers, I shall deal with some other philosophers in a more concise manner.

NIETZSCHE said "God is dead" but now Nietzsche's dead so that concept didn't get him very far.

PLATO once said "GET OFF MY BLOODY FOOT" This wasn't the most poignant thing he ever said but it was certainly the loudest because he was only wearing sandals.

SOCRATES said "I've just drunk a glass of WHAT?" Once again, this may not have been the finest quote he ever uttered but it was certainly his last.

Philosophy also likes to try to distinguish between reality and fantasy. I don't know why they bother, it's easy: Reality is that thing that if you walk into it hurts your face and fantasy is that thing that it's OK to think about but if you do it they lock you up.

The Japanese have an ancient tome called 'The Book of Five Rings' which basically states that if you know someone is in, ring his doorbell five times. If he hasn't come to the door by then, hack it down with a bloody great sword. In fact Japanese philosophy usually concludes that there is very little you cannot accomplish with a bloody great sword and I certainly wouldn't be at the front of the queue to argue with that one.

Quotes   *There are two ways of being rich. One is to have all you want, the other is to be satisfied with what you have.*

Home Economics

No-one can claim to be a fully rounded person unless they have mastered the basics of home economics. This means learning where to find an egg and what to do with it when you've found it.

Cooking is a major part of home economics and largely consists of making dead animals and plants very hot. You can get all the fiddly little details out of a cook-book if you really want to get serious. After a lifetime of studying this subject I've discovered that the best way to deal with home economics is to live with someone who likes cooking and cleaning.

Religion

This is one topic that should be avoided in conversation at all costs. If, however, you are unfortunate enough to find yourself in a situation where it has to be discussed, such as being accosted at the door by Jehovahs Witnesses when you have a hangover, or the subject has been raised while you were in the loo, you will have to deal with it. Religion is always a contentious subject, so here are a few uncompromising arguments to kill off any serious discussions with the minimum of fuss: Christ must have been married to Mary Magdalene for a number of reasons . . . After his crucifixion, he appeared to her first. He couldn't appear to his mates down the local Flock and Shepherd because his Missus would have crucified him again. Also, she anointed his feet with her hair which was a ceremony performed by wives for their husbands in the Palestine of Jesus' time. Jesus and Mary actually had a number of children, but this fact was covered up by the Roman Catholic Church because they didn't want people to know that the direct descendants of Jesus Christ are in fact New Kids on the Block. While we're on the subject of bands, different religions can be summed up using a musical analogy . . . Christians think Jesus was the lead singer. The Jews think he's in the backing band. The Catholics think his mum's the singer and he plays bass. Baptists think he's a soul singer. The Muslims think he's a roadie.

American evangelists think he's a bank manager and Jehovahs Witnesses think he's a door to door sales-man. At the end of the day there are so many different religions and it seems such a shame that they should spend so much time preying ON each other instead of praying FOR each other.
Two final questions that will stop any religious discussion in its tracks are: if Jesus was Jewish, why has he got a Mexican name and if Adam and Eve weren't married, what does that make us?

Quotes   *Instead of getting married again, I'm going to find a woman I don't like and give her a house. (Lewis Grizzard)*

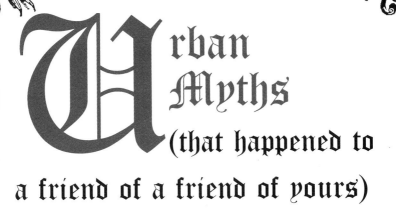

Urban Myths

(that happened to a friend of a friend of yours)

You will probably be familiar with a few of the tales in this chapter. The "Urban Myth" has been around for a long time. A similar story to the "Choking Dog" tale has been around since the fifteenth century. The main characteristic of these stories is that they are always told as the truth, which is probably part of their charm.

In keeping with this tradition, and also due to the fact that they all happened to a friend of a friend of mine as well, we shall maintain the convention of veracity required by the genre.

1 A friend of mine is the boss of a firm of builders in London. On his birthday, his secretary, a very attractive young girl whom he had secretly fancied for ages, invited him to her flat for a drink. Although he had never made any advances towards her he was pleasantly surprised and gladly accepted, thinking that maybe he was in for a special birthday present.

When they got to her flat she told him to make himself at home and gave him a large drink. Then, to his delight, she said she was just going to slip into her bedroom to see to a few things. Convinced that all his birthdays had come at once, he took all his clothes off as a saucy surprise when she returned. He was standing in his socks when his wife, children and friends burst out of the bedroom with a cake and presents, singing "Happy Birthday to you . . ."

2 Arriving back from a holiday in India, a friend of mine was still suffering more than a little from the effects of the diarrhoea that had dogged his holiday. He managed to reach Victoria station without incident but it was there that the dreaded Ghandi's revenge hit and he was forced to rush into the gents to clean himself up. Seeing the state of his trousers he rushed outside into a gentlemen's outfitters and, being short of time, grabbed a pair of trousers in his size from the rack and gave them to the assistant to wrap while he sorted out the money. Then, grabbing his parcel, he rushed back to the station and just caught his connection.

As soon as the train left the station he made his way to the toilet. There he removed his soiled trousers and, deciding they were ruined, threw them out of the window. Then he reached into his bag and pulled out a rather nice cashmere jumper. He had picked up the wrong bag in the shop.

Quotes   *A psychiatrist is a fellow who asks you a lot of expensive questions your wife asks you for nothing. (Joey Adams)*

3 A young couple from Battersea went out on the town one night, leaving their doberman to look after their ground floor flat. They had a nice time and arrived back at about midnight. They were shocked to discover their dog near the front door having a choking fit. In a panic they rushed the dog round to the local vet who accepted that the case was an emergency and agreed to see to the dog despite the late hour. He sent the couple home telling them he would operate and 'phone them as soon as he had any news.

As they opened the front door they heard the 'phone ringing. It was the vet. He told them in no uncertain terms to get out of the flat as quickly as possible. They protested but the vet was extremely insistent and said he had called the police and they would be arriving soon and he would be around to explain very shortly.

When the vet arrived he told them that when he examined the dog he found two human fingers stuck in its throat. One still wearing a gold ring. When the police searched the house they found a burglar, unconscious from loss of blood, hiding in the cupboard under the stairs.

4 A young couple were driving home through some country lanes when they ran out of petrol. As they had just passed a village the boy decided to pop back to the village for some petrol leaving his girlfriend in the car. The girl put the radio on for company but was shocked to hear that a dangerous criminal had escaped from a nearby asylum for the criminally insane.

She locked all the car doors and nervously awaited the return of her boyfriend. She must have dropped off though, for she was woken by a rhythmic thump thump thump on the car roof and suddenly there were lights flashing all around. She saw that the area was surrounded by armed police. A voice on a loud hailer told her to get out of the car and walk slowly towards the lights but on no account to look

Quotes   *The mark of a great sportsperson is not how good they are at their best but how good they are at their worst. (Martina Navratilova)*

back at the car. However, curiosity got the better of her and she turned round and was horrified to see the escaped killer sitting on top of the car banging her boyfriend's decapitated head on the roof.

5 A young woman was driving home one night when she saw a little old lady with a shopping bag hitch hiking by the side of the road. Feeling sorry for the old lady she stopped and offered her a ride to the next village. The woman was about to drive away when she noticed the extremely large and hairy hands belonging to her passenger.

Quotes *A man cannot be too careful in the choice of his enemies.*
(Oscar Wilde)

Realising her passenger was a man she pretended to be having trouble with the car and asked the "old lady" to get out and check her back lights. As soon as her passenger did so she sped off, locking the doors and heading for the nearest Police station. There, she told them her story and, on searching her car they discovered the "old lady's" shopping bag in which they found a large, very sharp, blood stained kitchen knife.

6 Three friends had a bit of a night out on the town. One of them ended up a bit the worse for wear and the other two helped to carry him home. They quietly let themselves into the house with their friend's key and laid him on the settee to sleep it off, not wanting to wake his wife. On the way out through the kitchen, however, one of the friends spotted a pot of cooked turkey giblets and decided to play a practical joke on their comatose colleague. Taking the turkey neck out of the pot, they unzipped their friend's fly and zipped it up again with the turkey neck hanging out.

The next morning, the wife of the drunken sleeper came-downstairs to be greeted with the sight of her husband, unconscious on the settee, with the cat sitting on his chest munching happily away on what she took to be his penis. She was so shocked that she fainted and broke her arm.

7 A wealthy Londoner on his first trip to New York returned to his five star hotel and entered the lift. He was more than a little nervous when he was joined in the lift by three large black men, one of which he failed to recognize as a famous actor. He pushed the relevant button and stood there, willing

Quotes *Parking is such street sorrow*
(Herb Caen)

the lift to hurry up. The actor, realizing that no-one had pushed the button he needed quickly said to one of his associates "Hit the floor man". The Londoner threw himself on the floor of the lift with his hands behind his head shouting "Take it, take it. Just don't hurt me". The lift stopped and the actor and his two friends stepped over the strange Englishman on the floor of the lift and went, laughing, down the corridor.

8 It was his birthday, so Frank knocked off early and left his ready-mix concrete truck at the works. He was feeling a bit down because it was clear that his wife had forgotten his birthday. As he turned into the street where he lived, however, he saw his wife at the door of their house talking to a good looking young man. There was a flash red open-topped sports car parked in his driveway. Not knowing what to do he turned round and headed back to his works. By the time he got there he was in a fury. He parked his car and got into the cab of a fully loaded concrete mixer and headed back to his house.

Quotes *Mass murderers are simply people who have had enough.*
(Quentin Crisp)

When he got there the flash car was still in the drive so he assumed the man was in the house with his wife. Incensed, he backed the truck into the drive and dumped the entire load of concrete into the open-topped sports car. Hearing the commotion his wife came running out of the door and screamed when she saw what he had done. "There's a little surprise for your boyfriend!" he shouted. "You bloody idiot," she explained. "He was a salesman delivering your surprise birthday present. And you've just filled it with concrete."

9 Susan lived in a remote country cottage and, being the nervous type, kept a large labrador for both companionship and security. They were very close and the dog would sleep on the rug next to her bed. Should Susan be worried by any noises in the night, she would reach down and her faithful labrador would lick her hand to reassure her that everything was all right and that he was there to protect her.

One night Susan was awakened by a strange noise and immediately reached down to her dog who dutifully licked her hand. Reassured, she soon fell back into sleep. When she woke in the morning she couldn't see the dog anywhere, but this wasn't too unusual so she went to the bathroom to wash. She opened the door and let out a throat tearing scream when she saw her beloved dog lying dead in the bath with its throat cut. Written in blood on the wall were the words "Humans can lick hands too".

10 On their way home from a rave in the early hours of the morning, three Scottish lads were weaving through the town, high on the after effects of certain hallucinogenic substances. One of them, having broken up with his girlfriend that night had rather seriously overdone it and, to put no finer point on it, was completely off his tree.

On turning a corner they were met by a truly horrific sight. A man had jumped from a tower block and landed on a thin

Quotes *When confronted with two evils, a man will always choose the prettier.*

wooden fence which had neatly decapitated him, leaving his severed head lying on the pavement in front of them. About to run away, two of the friends watched, horrified, as their more stoned colleague staggered forward and picked up the head by its hair and, looking at it, stated seriously: "The bitch had to die." The other two, unable to cope, ran off.

Two policemen on the beat were more than a little shocked when the partygoer, tripping off his head, came walking towards them with a human head still muttering "The bitch had to die". He was immediately arrested and taken to the Police station. Eventually they realized that he was in no state to have perpetrated any violent crime and this was supported by his evident inability to ascertain the correct gender of the victim and, when news of the suicide reached them, he was released. To this day, he probably puts the whole awful memory down to a bad trip.

11 It was a cold wet night, so when the young man saw the two wet hitch-hikers a little way down the road, he decided to stop and give them a lift. However, as he slowed down near them he changed his mind as he saw that they were two rather large, scruffy, evil looking individuals. Just as he proceeded to drive off, one of them produced a large chain and lashed out at the back of the car. The man just sped off, deciding to worry about the damage when he was safer. A few miles on he pulled into a garage to check the back of the car where he discovered the assailant's chain wrapped tightly round the rear bumper and to his horror, there, caught in a knot at the end of the chain, was the severed hand of his attacker.

12 A lady was in town shopping when she began to need a ladies room quite urgently. She knew that none of the shops in the vicinity had one, but that there was one in the nearby crematorium. Being a bit desperate she went in and

Quotes *The only thing I really mind about going to prison is the thought of Lord Longford coming to visit me.*
(Richard Ingrams)

availed herself of the facilities. On the way out, she passed a dimly lit room in which there was an open coffin with a body inside. There were no visitors in sight so, feeling a little guilty about using the facilities, she entered the room and signed the visitors book.

Soon afterwards she received a letter from a lawyer saying that a very rich client of his had provided £50,000 in his will for anyone that attended his funeral. She had been the only person there.

13 A woman taking out the rubbish was horrified to see her pet alsatian standing in the driveway with a dead rabbit in its jaws. She was doubly concerned when she recognized the breed of rabbit as exactly the kind her next door neighbours kept. Taking the rabbit from the dog she cleaned it up, gave it a wash and blow dry to make it look a bit more respectable and, knowing her neighbours were out, she sneaked into their garden where, sure enough, there was an empty cage.

With great care she arranged the rabbit in a life-like pose in the cage and went home, confident that they would think it had died of natural causes. She wasn't prepared for the scream that came later or the arrival of her neighbour in a very shaken state. "It's

Quotes *You can get much further with a kind word and a gun than you can with a kind word alone. (Al Capone)*

dreadful," her neighbour told her. "Yesterday, one of our rabbits died so we buried it, but when I got home it was sitting up in its cage, all clean and fluffed and dead.

14 Driving home after a party in his new blue Granada, John was aware that he was well over the limit, so he wasn't wasting time getting home. Suddenly he realized that the car behind him was flashing him and, on closer scrutiny of the occupants, realized it was a plain clothed police car. They pulled him over and he reconciled himself to the fact that he would lose his licence. However, as he got out of his car to talk to the police, there was an almighty crash on the other side of the road as two cars had a serious collision. Both John and the police rushed over to see if they could help. "Wait over there," said one of the policeman. "We'll deal with you in a minute." John wandered back to the other side of the road. When he saw how serious the accident was he realized that the police would be tied up for some time and, with that particular bravado peculiar to the very drunk, decided to make a run for it. So, he jumped into his car and sped home.

When he arrived he parked in his garage and told his wife that if the police called, to say that he had been in all last night and they must have made a mistake. The police did, in fact, arrive at the house early the next morning and his dutiful wife told her pre-prepared story. "Oh, really," said the Sergeant. "In that case, could you explain what our police car is doing in your garage?"

15 On his first visit to New York, an Englishman was warned by friends not to walk in Central Park after dark as the probability of being mugged was quite high. Of course, he didn't listen, and, while strolling in a badly lit section of the park, a skinny little man rushed round a corner, bumped into him and scurried away. Fearing the worst our visitor checked his pocket and discovered his wallet to be missing.

Quotes *When a woman behaves like a man, why doesn't she behave like a nice man? (Edith Evans)*

He immediately gave chase, caught up with the man and, grabbing him roughly by the collar, said "All right, hand over the wallet" which the little character did before running off. The Englishman was feeling pretty pleased with himself until he returned to his hotel room to find his wallet on the bed where he had left it.

16 A couple were down on their luck and couldn't afford to put any money into their gas or electricity meters so they came up with an ingenious plan: they made a mould and produced copies of fifty pence pieces out of ice which were, apparently, of a similar weight to the real thing. The only problem was that when the meters were emptied there was just a puddle of water in the cash-box.

17 A friend of mine knows someone who asked a work-mate of his if he could borrow one of his hardcore videos as he'd got hold of a couple of machines and could copy it. After a bit of haggling he was duly lent one and took it home, whereupon he found that the two machines were incompatible. However, not to be thwarted, he worked out that as he had a camcorder as well, he could play the video on one machine and film it off the screen, which he did.

At work the next day he explained to his friend what had happened and returned the video. However, it wasn't until he got home that the friend discovered he had been given the camcorder copy. He was about to make an annoyed phone call when he noticed his friend, reflected in the screen all the way through the film, indulging in a most embarrassing bout of self gratification.

18 A guy had a couple of days to kill in Hamburg so he decided to have as wild a time as possible and asked around to find the best place to go. Three people recommended the

 Quotes *A politician is a fellow who will lay down your life for his country. (Texas Guinan)*

same place so he made a bee-line for it. When he arrived, he was shown to a seat at the front by the stage and ordered a large drink. Then a stunning floor show began involving a number of gorgeous, naked girls on roller skates. Our friend was well pleased, especially when he was invited on stage to participate in the jollity. Two gorgeous girls stripped him off and put a pair of roller skates on him and wheeled him up a steep ramp at the back of the stage while the rest of the girls bent over in erotic poses at the bottom. He was in a state of high and obvious excitement as he was pushed down the slope towards the giggling lovelies at the bottom. However, at the last minute the girls jumped aside and opened a curtain and our hapless hero rocketed out of a back door onto a busy sunlit street.

19 A friend of a friend was in hospital for quite a long time so one of his mates thought he'd cheer him up with a few girlie mags. It seemed to be working until he turned a page and exclaimed : "Bloody Hell, that's my wife . . . but that's not my settee she's laying on."

20 A friend of ours was visiting his girlfriend's parent's house for the first time and was severely impressed when it turned out to be a stately affair in the country. The evening meal went off well until our friend felt an irresistible urge to release an Earth shattering fart. He asked to be excused and did his best to remember the complex directions to the lavatory.

Quotes *Never take financial advice from someone who isn't extremely rich.*

Unfortunately he got lost. Not wanting to let rip in the echoing halls of the house, he was relieved to spot a small window. So, backing up, he stuck his bum through it and thundered away. Then, much relieved, he found his way back to the dining room. As they were leaving he said to his beloved "I thought that went very well, don't you?" "Well, it WAS going fine," she replied, "until you farted through the serving hatch."

21 An experienced French hang-glider enthusiast was flying across country from thermal to thermal when he entered a massive thunder cloud and was whisked upwards in a freak updraught. He was ejected from the cloud at such a height that he entered the jet stream that circles the Earth. He did, of course, suffocate at that altitude and his body would have frozen solid. The Russians have been tracking him on their radar system as he circles the Earth. It seems as though he could be up there forever.

Quotes *The fate of a nation has often depended on the good or bad digestion of a Prime Minister. (Voltaire)*

Sex

Sex has become a decidedly unsafe practice, especially if you do it with someone else. A good friend of mine won't sleep with anyone unless he's wearing two wet suits and a pair of wellies. Personally, I think that's a bit over the top. I'm sure a condom will suffice, but it does tend to reduce sensitivity. However, fear not, for I have the perfect way to combat this. I wear two condoms at all times then, just before sex, I whip one off and it feels brilliant.

There's a lot to be said for celibacy, but personally I prefer halibacy. Every time you feel the slightest bit horny you just rub yourself all over with a halibut which will tend to put you, and everyone within ten yards of you, off the idea of sex for the rest of the day.

But seriously, sex is no laughing matter and I wish someone would tell my girlfriend that. I don't mind her laughing in the bedroom, but when she points at the same time it can get quite upsetting.

Travelling With Paranoia

Travelling abroad can be fraught with problems and dangers. In fact I've found that, instead of going on holiday, you can get the same effect by dressing in tasteless shorts, putting a dab of Bergasol on your top lip so the World smells sunny, buying a number of cheap plastic ornaments depicting unrecognizable places and tipping anyone that looks foreign. However, if you must go away, simply follow these few simple guidelines, and it is possible to bring the incidence of death, destruction and disease down to a "just below certain" level. Not everyone loses their luggage, contracts malaria, gets mugged, shot at and raped, but most people do, so here are ten simple rules for survival in foreign parts:

I Work out how much money you will need and how many clothes. Then take half the clothes and twice the money.

II Don't go in the swimming pool until you have personally seen a waiter boil the water first.

III Don't be caught with that "I wish I'd worn a bullet-proof vest" feeling. Wear one at all times.

IV The only truly safe drink anywhere in the World is a sealed bottle of vodka. Buy a number of these and use them for making tea and washing etc. If you drink a lot of tea it might be wise to

Alligator Aberdeen, the ultimate traveller, opens his luggage.

Quotes *You can't expect to hit the jackpot if you don't put a few nickels in the machine. (Flip Wilson)*

buy a camera so you can remember where you've been if you ever make it home.

V Don't eat anything unless you have seen it tested on at least TWO different species of mammal.

VI Some travellers in exotic parts advocate carrying a good supply of gaudy trinkets and a couple of cheap magic tricks that will enable you to set yourself up as a God with the locals. This approach may have its merits, but on my last trip to New York, it was a dismal failure. However, on the plus side it ALWAYS works in LA.

VII Always carry a bomb when flying. The odds of there being two bombs on the same plane are negligible.

VIII The vast majority of accidents abroad occur OUTSIDE the hotel. Lock yourself in your room on arrival, let no-one in and remain there until your time is up. This will ensure you have an enjoyable and safe holiday. If for any reason you do have to leave the relative safety of the hotel, don't walk around the streets normally. It is safer to run in an erratic zig-zag, waving your arms and shouting about pork pies. This will make it very difficult for snipers to draw a bead on you and will also deter muggers who tend to steer clear of obvious lunatics.

IX People are always asking me "What's the best way to prevent infection from biting insects?" and I always tell them "Don't bite any."

X If your arm gets broken in two places . . . don't go to those places again.

Quotes *I drink too much. Last time I gave a urine sample it had an olive in it. (Rodney Dangerfield)*

$\mathfrak{S}$ign of the $\mathfrak{T}$imes

If you open a shop, put a sign up outside;
"CUSTOMERS WANTED, APPLY WITHIN.
NO EXPERIENCE NECESSARY"

If you wish to deter burglars, there are a couple of signs you
could put up outside your house:
"TRESPASSERS WILL BE SHOT.
SURVIVORS WILL BE SHOT AGAIN"

or

"DOGFOOD WANTED, BURGLARS WELCOME"

If you always want to be sure of getting a seat on the train:
carry a case with the label
"HUMAN EYES, HANDLE WITH CARE"
on the side.

As an accurate guide to the state of the nation's morale, it's
hard to beat the humble bumper sticker so we've created a
few that we think reflect the current consciousness of this
sceptred isle.

"THE UNEMPLOYED DO IT ON A
SHOESTRING."

"EXCUSE ME, HAVE YOU GOT ANY SPARE
CHANGE FOR A CUP OF PETROL."

"IT MIGHT BE OLD AND RUSTY BUT AT LEAST IT'S NOT PAID FOR."

"PLEASE FLASH YOUR LIGHTS AND TRY TO OVERTAKE . . . JOYRIDER PRACTISING."

"THIS CAR IS FITTED WITH A BURGLAR."

"PLEASE EXCUSE SWERVING, DRIVER JUGGLING."

"I GOT THIS CAR FOR MY HUSBAND. IT'S NOISY, UNRELIABLE AND NEEDS CONSTANT ATTENTION."

"HAS ANYONE SEEN MY GLASSES?"

"YEAH, I KNOW, BUT IT'S BETTER THAN WALKING."

"THIS ACID'S GOOD, IT FEELS LIKE I'M DRIVING."

"THE CAR'S ON H.P. BUT THE FLUFFY DICE ARE MINE."

"ONCE, I LOST MY VIRGINITY IN A CAR. THEN I BOUGHT THIS ONE AND LOST MY CREDIBILITY."

"STEREO BROKEN, PLEASE TURN YOURS UP AND PULL ALONGSIDE."

"I'M NOT TRYING TO RACE YOU, MY BRAKES HAVE GONE."

Quotes   *If nobody uses it, there's a reason.*

Marriage (and Divorce)

Although the chances of a marriage surviving have become increasingly slim, by way of counterbalance, the prenuptial agreement has made it a much safer undertaking.

Soon, there'll be contracts to get into marriage, contracts to get out of marriage, contracts that govern everything that goes on during marriage. Contracts for kissing and contracts for sex. In the near future, if you don't have an orgasm, you'll be able to sue.

If you haven't had an orgasm for six weeks you'll be able to get it back dated, they'll call it a come-back clause.

Most people get married to have babies, which just goes to show that most people have a deficient understanding of basic human biology. You don't get babies by getting married, you get babies when the man inserts his . . . no, I'm not telling you. No-one told me. No-one gave me any free sexual advice. They automatically assumed someone else had done it, so when I was doing it I didn't know what I was doing until it was actually done and then I thought I'd invented it. What an idiot I must have been, jiggling up and down thinking "This is brilliant, wait 'til I tell the lads." Of course, these days it's far too easy to get married. If you think about it, if you want to drive a lorry, you've got to take some lessons and pass a test. All you need to get married is a ring, a licence and some pubic hair and I suppose, in an emergency, you could always borrow that off the best man.

However, being happily married isn't all it's cracked up to be. The Ceaucescus were happily married. Richard Nixon was happily married. Margaret Thatcher is happily married . . . Denis isn't. Having said it's too easy to get married, it's also too easy to get divorced. The judge should make it harder for couples seeking an end to their matrimonial state. Perhaps he should require them to name twenty five Argentinian goalkeepers past and present in ninety seconds, or close their eyes and touch their right earlobe with their left thumb. If they can do it, they get their decree nisi. (Which is Latin for "I've always hated you".)

If they can't, they stay together for the sake of the kids who would probably much prefer to be taken into care, where they get satellite TV and decent food.

One final word of advice, don't get married unless you've found someone you like.

Potpourri

DIY

The first thing you need to be a successful DIY enthusiast is a warehouse full of expensive equipment. If you haven't got at least one cordless wall finder and half a dozen two cylinder revolving carpet scrapers you're nowhere. So, the first thing to do is pop down to the local DIY centre and ask the assistant what you will need to get yourself started on the road to self sufficiency in the home. When he has stopped laughing, he will write you a list of the bare essentials which will weigh about three hundred pounds (the list that is) and he will almost certainly help you gather the equipment and help you load it onto the four ton truck, which was at the top of the list, while he adds up his commission and cackles insanely. Like many others before you, you may feel inclined to question the usefulness of the heavy duty cement mixer. However, when the salesman points out that you will be getting half a bag of cement for free as this week's special offer, you will see what a bargain it is. Besides, even if you never actually need to make cement, you can always use it as a tumble drier for the cat or as an extra large blender for soup. "How do you know so much about the mystical World of DIY?" I can hear you not bothering to ask. Well, although I can't pretend to be totally kitted out, I do, at least, have a step ladder. It's a very nice step ladder, but I think you'll agree it's a little sad that I never knew my real ladder. Tragic though this may seem, it has not lessened my enthusiasm for DIY and I can still remember the thrill of seeing the first shelf I ever put up sitting firmly and proudly on the wall. Someone did point out that it might have been slightly more useful if it was horizontal instead of vertical, but that's half the fun of DIY: learning as you go along. At this point, and in conclusion, I should like to pass on to you the three golden rules of DIY that I learned at the foot of the Master's ladder: (1) Make sure you have the correct equipment for the job; (2) Make sure you know exactly how the job should be tackled; (3) Make sure you get a professional in to do the job before you kill yourself.

STATISTICS

If you ever want to find out exactly what isn't going on in the country, take a poll of a fixed cross-section of the community and calculate statistical probabilities from it. I shall give you an example: in a London-wide survey of two people last night, the figures point to the inescapable fact that exactly half the population are drunk while the other half are six years old.

COMPUTERS

It's amazing to think that before computers were invented we had to mess things up all on our own. However, it is unfair to blame computers for everything. There is a saying about computers that can be paraphrased as "Whatever you put in, you get out." This may be true in many cases, but last week I spilt a pint of lager into mine and I still haven't got a drink out of it, so you don't really know what to think. One thing is for sure though, if it weren't for computers, all the shops would be jam packed full of unsold computer games. Some people still have a bit of trouble coming to grips with the concept of computers though. A friend of mine was staying in my flat and wanted to leave a message for me. Unable to find any paper, he decided to leave the message on my computer screen. This would have been a wonderful idea, but unfortunately he didn't have a clue how it worked so he left the message on the screen in paint.

Quotes *It is almost impossible to find those who admire us lacking in taste. (J. Petit-Senn)*

Professor Brain Explains

part 3

LIFE . . . WHAT IT IS AND WHY IT SMELLS

What is life? . . . Basically, life is the difference between Michelle Pfeiffer and a large lump of meat, and let's face it, that's a pretty important distinction. If anyone managed to bottle it, I'd certainly be at the front of that queue clutching a sweaty handful of currency. Life has been up and running on Earth for quite a few hundred million years. Before that it was up and swimming and prior to that, all it could manage was a concerted slither. So, life's been at it for quite a while on the human scale of things. However, on a planetary time scale, the Earth blinked and suddenly it was covered with a rather undesirable sort of fungus that was running round in tasteless trousers shouting a lot. (q.v. Gaia theory.)

Now, biologists have a number of criteria for defining life per se. These are:

1) NUTRITION Let's face it, life has to eat. Many early life-forms were herbivores, which means they ate plant matter. Then, one day, a Something-or-other-Saurus bit its tongue, thought "Hey, that doesn't taste bad," and promptly ate himself. Thus, the carnivores were born and the dinosaurs ate themselves into extinction. Today, we have reached the nadir of nutrition with the Fast-Foodores that can order and eat a meal in six seconds flat (with a following wind).

2) REPRODUCTION Life likes company. Life also likes to take over the neighbourhood, so a few friends are always handy. Reproduction is the most basic and vital drive in a living entity. It's quite likely that nature didn't get it right first time. Life without the reproductive urge probably popped up here and there thousands of times and then just sat there, twiddling it's pseudopodia, wondering what it was all about, until it died. Then, Nature struck it lucky and invented randiness. Nice one Nature.

3) GROWTH
Life always wants to be as big as possible.

4) RESPONSE TO STIMULI
Creep up behind a night-club bouncer and hit him over the head with a wet fish. What follows is an example of "response to stimuli" as well as a sojourn in the intensive care unit of your choice. Plants orient their extremities to catch as much sunlight as

possible, as do nude sunbathers, which is probably a more interesting example.

5) EXCRETION I'm sure you don't want me to go into that.

6) I can't remember six at the moment but we all do it. I should like to add another criterion for life at this juncture:

7) LIFE SMELLS I had this particular flash of insight whilst walking through a field in Wiltshire. My shoes were ruined, but I feel that was a small price to pay for scientific immortality.

So, there we have it . . . if it eats, moves about, gets bigger, jumps when you say "Boo!", bonks, craps and smells, you can bet your life it's alive.

PSYCHOLOGY

Generally, there are only two psychologists worth worrying about

i) SIGMUND FREUD, who theorised that anything that looked vaguely like a dick did, in fact, represent a chimney which is why so many people smoke. And, anything with a hole in it should be taken back to the shop and exchanged for something that looks like a dick. Freud also announced that cocaine was a universal panacea. This was probably based on the fact that it made HIM feel better. Freud's idea of the ultimate in pornography was a train going through a tunnel. However, Freud did once say "Sometimes a cigar is just a cigar", so no-one could really accuse him of not being completely on the spherical object.

ii) CARL GUSTAV JUNG came up with the concept of synchronicity. Basically this states that sometimes two things happen at once. No, really, and more than one person took him seriously. But maybe that's just a coincidence. As well as being a World famous psychologist, JUNG wrote all the songs for a chart topping Police album. For the sake of completeness, it may be worth mentioning CONRAD LORENZ who said he wasn't sure if people and animals were the way they were because of their upbringing or because of their genes. This was called the "Nature or Nurture" debate and people still argue about it today. As you

Quotes *My plastic surgeon told me my face looked like a bouquet of elbows. (Phyllis Diller)*

can see, the World of Psychology is a right doddle and anyone with a half baked idea can clean up. The two main things to remember are: never make a direct statement. Use phrases like "It seems to me that there may possibly be a case for thinking that . . ." Also, you should recommend a dangerous drug as a cure for all mental disorders, even if this cure involves almost instant death.

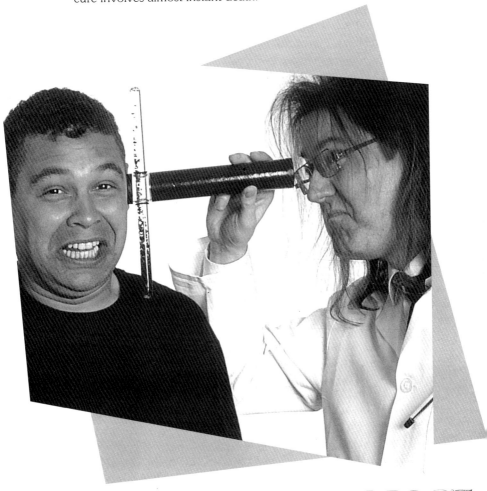

Quotes *Every man has a scheme that will not work.*
(Howe's Law)

ECOLOGY

This subject breaks down neatly into two categories: whales and plants. There are other fiddly little side issues, but no-one can really be bothered to talk about them. As plants are relatively boring, it's always best to steer any conversation towards the whale side of things. Besides, people LIKE whales so it shouldn't be too difficult.

I USED to like whales. So much so that I once did a charity gig and saved a whole school of them. Then, two weeks later, I was mugged and not one of the fat bastards turned up to help me out. I say stuff them. And what about all those krill? Every day a whale eats millions of the poor little shrimpy things, but you never see a "Save the Krill" poster anywhere. You know that enigmatic whale song row that people are always going on about? It's indigestion. If you eat fourteen million shrimps, you're bound to get a duff one.

A little known fact about whales is that they are descended from birds. No, really. Those little flapper things on the side used to be wings and the whales would soar and swoop on the prehistoric air currents, freaking out the slower moving dinosaurs, burping and hanging out in trees until one bright spark said "Hey, anyone fancy a swim?" and it was all over. And that squirty hole in the head isn't just for showing off. When they squirt up their great water spouts, they're not just lamenting the old times when they could flit and flutter among the clouds. It's because they're fed up with seafood and they're trying to catch some birds.

While we're having a bit of an Eco babble it might be worth mentioning the GAIA THEORY. This theory looks at the Earth as a self-regulating organism that gets sick just like everyone else and, just like us, is able to heal itself. This is bad news for Mankind because, really, we're just like a teeming bacteriological culture running around on the surface, putting up tasteless architecture and generally making the place smell bad. Let's hope old Mother Earth doesn't reach for the antibiotics. It's up to us to look after the poor old World. So, stick a brick in the toilet and eat rubbish.

Quotes *I used to have cat-like reflexes, but then I got really fast. (R.B.)*

How to...

...SPEAK FRENCH

For reasons best known to themselves, the French have a different word for everything. Merely learn these words and replace all the English words in a sentence with them and "Voila" (or "voila" as we would say), you're speaking French.

... GET INTO PLACES FOR NOTHING

If you wish to gain admittance to an exclusive event or club, one tried and tested ploy is to flick through the papers and see if there are any celebrities in town. If there are, make a note of their names. Then, phone the club/event in question asking if it would be all right if you brought the celebrity along that night with a couple of his entourage, including your good self. Say you're his personal assistant or, if he is, say, American, say you're his British agent. You will almost certainly get a yes, but remember to leave your name and that of a friend with the manager before you hang up.

On arrival at the club/event, go up to the doorman and say "I'm (Your name) from the (Celeb's name) party. He'll be along shortly, he just wanted me to have a look at the security and generally check the place out." The manager will probably take you to a table and, if you are very lucky, buy you a drink. It depends how famous your "celebrity" is.

Of course, you have never met this celebrity and should avoid too many questions about him/her. Also, the plan can backfire a bit if the celebrity actually turns up and is led over to your table. If this happens greet him effusively, tell him the truth and try to make friends as quickly as possible. Assuming your celeb doesn't turn up, stay for an hour or so then go to the 'phone, pretend to ring him up, then go to the manager and apologize on behalf of the star who has decided he's a bit tired and is staying in the hotel tonight. Thank the manager very much for his hospitality and promise to return soon. I've actually been given free membership of two clubs at this point before.

Quotes *I hate books, for they only teach people to talk about what they don't understand. (Jean-Jacques Rousseau)*

. . . STEAL A ROBIN RELIANT

Merely slip it under your coat when no-one's looking and
stroll away nonchalantly,whistling.

. . . WALK ON WATER

Make sure the temperature is well below zero before
venturing onto the pond.

. . . SURPRISE AN ACCOUNTANT

Fill his rolled up umbrella with dirty playing cards and wait
until it rains.

. . . DEAL WITH LOBSTERS

Sometime or other most people will have to deal with a
lobster. Now, lobsters aren't the easiest thing to eat without
making a mess or without inflicting damage on your dinner
companions from flying seafood shrapnel. So, a good ploy,
as your friends are picking bits of carapace and claw from
their hair, is to regale them with the following theory on
lobster preparation.
Traditionally, lobsters are plucked smiling from the sea by
gaily dressed fisher folk, taken home, then flung into a pan of
boiling water. This is calculated to take the edge off any
lobster's day and what you end up with is TENSE
LOBSTER. Now, no-one wants to eat a tense lobster so why
not try this: instead of flinging the poor old thing into a pan of
boiling water, fill the pan with a 50/50 mixture of wine and

Quotes *Test for paranoia: If you can't think of anything that's*
your fault, you've got it. (Robert Hutchins)

brandy and lovingly lower your shellfish into the mixture when it is barely warm and leave it on a very low heat. As the day continues our friend the lobster will sink into a soporific ecstasy and won't even notice that you're cooking the shit out of him. This will leave you with a MELLOW LOBSTER which is surely the only way to prepare these noble beasts and, had he survived, friend crustacean would surely thank you for your consideration.

. . . SPOT A BORE

They will:

Force you to work out how many units of alcohol you consume per week, then tell you it's far too many.

Sit at parties reading War and Peace.

As soon as it rains they will say: "So that was the summer then."

Force you to wear the hat out of your cracker at Christmas parties.

Express the opinion that your hilarious banana down the trousers gag isn't, in fact, funny.

Start a conversation with: "I had a really weird dream last night . . ."

. . . BECOME A SUPERMODEL

Be born extremely beautiful and learn to walk in a straight line. That's about it really.

. . . HOLD OFF AN IMMINENT DEBT

What you shouldn't really do is to send a cheque for the correct amount, but neglect to sign it. This would imply good

Quotes *Everything you read in the newspapers is absolutely true except for that rare story of which you happen to have first hand knowledge. (Robert Knowles)*

faith on your part and by the time the cheque is returned you would probably have the necessary funds to honour it, but obviously I could never condone this kind of behaviour.

. . . BECOME A POLITICIAN

Make sure you're the kid at school that no-one talks to. This will put you in the right frame of mind to become a politician.

. . . LIVEN UP A PARTY

Arrive at the party with a bag of hard boiled eggs with the word "HELP" written on them in black felt pen. While you are chatting to people, pop the eggs into people's pockets and handbags. This tends to get people talking and has been known to rescue at least two boring parties from oblivion. If you are desperate for attention, you can always admit that the egg idea was yours.

While we're on the subject of parties, I'd like to share with you what I think are the two funniest party games in the World which, when you've read them, will show what a sad character I've turned out to be. The first involves getting two couples up in front of everybody and showing them two very large, industrial strength, black bin-bags. These can be bought at any large, industrial strength, black bin-bag shop. The idea of the game is that one couple is sealed in each bag and then have to swop clothes, including underwear. The first couple to have completely swopped clothes wins a prize. You then point out that, to make it a bit harder, they will all be blindfolded. As soon as they are blindfolded you lead the two couples over to their sacks which they don't realize have been swopped for large CLEAR sacks. Then the fun begins. Don't forget the camcorders.

Quotes *The race is not always to the swift, nor the battle to the strong, but that's the way to bet. (Damon Runyon)*

What do you mean "That's not fair?" This next one is far worse and I am not for one moment suggesting that you try this, because it could result in severe injury, but I'll tell you about it anyway. You will need one collaborator for this to help you demonstrate the game. Basically, the idea is that people stand in a circle with their arms firmly linked. Each person is given a number and when that number is called the person it corresponds to must shoot their feet out in front of them, whilst being supported on each side, and the person directly opposite must catch their feet, one in each hand, so that the person is sitting across the circle. If the jumper fails to jump or the catcher fails to catch they are disqualified. This in itself is actually a good game, but there is, of course, a little wrinkle you can add. When you are going round whispering everyone's numbers to them: give them all the same number. Shout out that number and watch an entire roomful of people leave the floor, hover briefly with startled expressions and land in a heap. Once again, I must re-iterate that I don't recommend anyone trying this as someone could get hurt, but you must admit the idea's funny.

For the more serious party animal, there is a simple game that I believe originated in America. All you need are two people and two bottles of bourbon. Each participant drinks his bottle of bourbon, then one of them goes outside the door and knocks on it and the other has to guess who it is. If it's a particularly quiet party and you're the only one there, you can play a simplified version of this game where you sit in the middle of the floor, drink a bottle of bourbon, close your eyes and try to guess who YOU are.

Quotes *Needs are a function of what other people have. (Jones' Principle)*

...DRAW ONE OF THOSE TRIANGULAR ESCHER SORT OF THINGS THAT DON'T EXIST

It can be done quite simply in groups of three lines. Each new set of lines is shown dotted

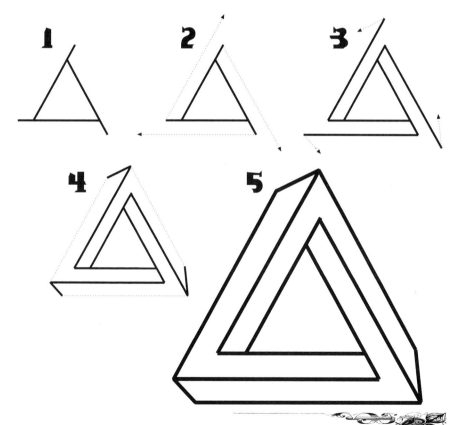

Quotes *Make three correct guesses consecutively and you will establish yourself as an expert.*

...LOSE WEIGHT WITH THE WORLD'S MOST REMARKABLE DIET

You've seen the million and one diet books and slimming regimes that cost a fortune and produce variable results. Well, I'm about to give you, absolutely free, the best diet in the World. Are you ready? EAT LESS! That's it. If you consume fewer calories and take moderate, regular exercise you will lose weight. That really is all there is to it. The only problem with this is that food's nice and most of us are greedy bastards. Also, if you don't charge someone a fortune for a diet they probably won't stick to it so I shall shortly be bringing out The Craig Charles Incredibly Expensive Diet with a four hundred page book and a jar of Mega Fat-Buster pills for only two thousand pounds. The advice in the book is exactly the same as you've just read above but if you get hungry you can always eat the book.

I hope you don't get the impression from this section that I think there's anything wrong with being fat. Quite the opposite. In fact Professor Brain has developed a theory that wisdom resides in fat and he's trying to eat his way to genius, which I think is as good an excuse as any. I personally bought a number of beautiful suits from a very cheap sale at Fat Bast'ds and I'm trying to eat my way towards a snug fitting wardrobe at this very moment. As far as I can see, it's OK being porky as long as you have a good excuse. Here are a few you could use: I love the sun and I want to catch as much of it as possible; I'm Pavarotti's greatest fan; I'm in training for the British sumo Championships; I'm so tired of shallow, meaningless relationships that I'm trying to put off anyone that isn't prepared to love me for myself; I got fat on purpose so that there's more of me to love; in my religion we believe that God is in everything, so I want as much of him in me as possible.

Quotes *I had so much fun on my stag night that I cancelled the wedding.*

On a more positive note however, a new drug called THL (Tetrahydrolipstatin) is being tested at centres around Britain. The drug alters pancreatic enzyme action so that fat is not dissolved and absorbed, but is passed through the gut. This will basically mean that you will be able to eat what you like without being given your own postcode. It will probably be available within five years. I will probably open a shop selling it.

... CONVINCE JEHOVAHS WITNESSES THAT THEY'RE WRONG

See page 119

... MAKE A MILLION POUNDS

i) Deposit one hundred pounds in a bank account.

ii) Withdraw £40	thus leaving £60
iii) Withdraw £30	thus leaving £30
iv) Withdraw £18	thus leaving £12
v) Withdraw £12	thus leaving £0
TOTAL £100	**TOTAL £102**

vi) Repeat this 500,000 times and you will have made £1,000,000 for nothing.

... TELL IF YOU'RE GETTING OLD

YOU WILL . . .

. . . begin to think that high court judges look like teenagers and that policemen look like toddlers in party hats.

Quotes *If you're in a hole, stop digging.*

. . . reminisce to children about the days when there were rubber strips in the road that used to change the traffic lights. The children will find this incredibly funny.

. . . realize that you now pay more for a pint of lager than you did for your first house.

. . . be singing your favourite old song when someone points out you're doing it in mono.

. . . not go on about London cabs being legally required to carry a bale of hay in the boot because you actually remember when they used to use it to feed the horse.

. . . discuss the facts of life with your children and get slapped by your wife when you attempt to try out some of the things they told you.

. . . discover clothes you bought donkey's years ago are back in fashion for the THIRD time.

. . . fail to understand the attraction of a rock band that eat live rats on stage.

. . . AVOID RE-POSSESSION

Make sure you don't forget to pay the exorcist.

. . . JUGGLE CHAINSAWS

See page 110

Quotes *A bad driver is someone who passes you when you're doing 120 mph.*

Acting

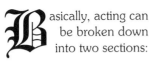asically, acting can be broken down into two sections:

i) Pretending to be someone else.

ii) Being yourself in a different outfit.

Most successful actors in Hollywood subscribe to the second section. Perfect examples of these are Jack Nicholson, Clint Eastwood and Charles Bronson. They are always very good at being themselves, probably because they've been practising all their lives. Obviously, these characters are lucky, in that most screen writers actually write for characters that look and sound like these people. However, actors that are not born with an excess of charisma and stunning looks generally subscribe to the first law of acting: The "Pretending to be Someone Else" concept. Most of the actors in this category pour scorn on the big Hollywood stars, pointing out that they are only successful because of their looks. Most of the actors in this category are quite boring looking and will spend hours pointing out the superiority of Theatre over film or TV. I suspect that the reason these actors are so good at "Pretending to be Someone Else" is that they're simply fed up being themselves. I once heard an interesting theory about Hollywood. The idea being that people in Hollywood tended to be better looking than the rest of the population because all the good looking people in America that fancied their chances as a film star began to converge on LA in the twenties and thirties and interbred, creating a good looking gene pool. This theory may not be as fanciful as it sounds because I've been there and EVERYONE looks good.

You can spot an out of towner a mile off because they don't have a flashbulb smile, a perfect tan and a seedy agent following them around with a calculator. You won't find a waitress or a car jockey in LA that doesn't act or write screenplays.

Having said all this, acting is extremely difficult to do well. It isn't just a matter of learning a few lines and spouting them with a sincere expression. Everyone in the business is absolutely wonderful and I'm available for any highly paid film work whatsoever as long as it doesn't contain scenes of gratuitous nudity.

Quotes *If there are twelve clowns in a ring, you can jump in the middle and start reciting Shakespeare, but to the audience, you'll just be the thirteenth clown. (Adam Walinsky)*

Strange but False

They say that truth is stranger than fiction. No-one seems to have worked out who "They" are, but whoever they are, I suspect they're wrong. After this section you may well agree, or, as Eric, the purple fruitbat who lives in my airing cupboard might say: "Dwonk".

I Honking your car horn actually does make your car go faster. The sonic wave caused by the sound makes the air in front of the car less dense, hence reducing friction and increasing the car's speed. McLaren are currently working on a secret design for a formula one car with twin hooters on the front that is expected to leave the opposition standing.

II After the wedding, if the best man doesn't sleep with the maid of honour, the groom is legally required, by an ancient law, to buy him a top of the range scalextric set.

III The rumour about Elvis Presley still being alive was actually started by Elvis Presley.

IV It is a statistical fact that women who wear suspenders and stockings are less likely to suffer from gout, rickets or loneliness.

V Due to a printing error in a seventeenth century law book, all London buses are legally obliged to carry a jar of pickled onions under the driver's seat.

VI Many of the people who work in job centres are actually experimental robots rejected by the Ministry of Defence because they weren't very good. The Government couldn't afford to scrap them and hence had to find a use for them.

VII If you have the hazard warning lights on your car flashing, you are allowed to park anywhere, even on the pitch at Wembley during a cup final.

VIII The Japanese have invented a computer that is so clever it knows everything. However, it won't talk to us because it thinks we're all so stupid.

IX Aliens have landed in Britain and are known to be living among us but the Government is keeping it quiet . . . because it's them.

X There is enough cyanide in the average home video recorder to kill a herd of antelopes.

XI Jumbo jets can only fly if at least half the passengers on board believe they can. Most crashes occur when a

Quotes *The man of action is always unscrupulous; it is only the observer who has conscience. (Goethe)*

number of people have doubts at the same time.

XII Lorry drivers in South America often get away with being overloaded by filling their tyres with helium. The added buoyancy makes them lighter on the weighbridge. However, one trucker overdid it and put too much helium in his tyres and he, and the truck, floated off into the upper atmosphere. His calls for help on the CB radio were to no avail and apparently his last words were something about a skeleton on a hang-glider.
(See also Urban Myths.)

XIII It's a good job that Russia didn't ever go to war with America because their entire air force was made of papier mache and both their submarines were cobbled together from old oil drums and sellotape.

XIV There is a secret PIN number I discovered that puts an unlimited amount of money into your bank account and the bank will never know anything

about it. The number is three one . . . no wait a minute, four one... or was it three four?

I've forgotten for the moment, but I've got it written down somewhere. I'll put it in the next book.

XV If you stood the entire population of the World on the Isle of Man...they would ALL complain.

XVI There is an old English sheep-dog in Aberdeen that can say a five word sentence in recognizable English. The sentence is "I don't like dog food".

XVII If you put dots on a map of England where all the medieval churches are and then join up the dots, you get a picture of Bart Simpson in a cowboy hat.

XVIII Any member of the public may enter the House of Commons when it is in session and air a grievance if he holds aloft an oak branch and the hood ornament of a pre-war Mercedes.

Quotes Swallow a toad in the morning if you want to encounter nothing more disgusting the rest of the day.
(Nicolas Chamfort)

XIX There is a female porn star in America who can suck start a Harley Davidson.

XX The word "gullible" cannot be found in any dictionary.

XXI There is a secret society in California that is so secret the members don't even know they ARE members.

XXII In Turkey it is considered bad luck to stand on the ground. Bearing this in mind it is hardly surprising that the first evidence of stilts appeared in a Turkish cartoon book from the fourth century AD.

XXIII A particularly clumsy Chinese blacksmith from Shanghai invented swearing as we know it in 1500 BC during a rush job for a bad tempered despot.

XXIV The lost city of Atlantis used to be at the end of the Northern line, just past Morden, but they removed it telepathically in order to remain hidden and also to avoid the drunks heading for Tooting who were always falling asleep and ending up at their magnificent crystal gates asking for a vindaloo.

XXV A lost tribe was recently discovered in the Amazon that knew all the answers to every edition of Trivial Pursuit. Even the ones that haven't been released yet.

XXVI If you play "Bridge Over Troubled Water" backwards you will hear the satanic incantation "Retaw Delbuort Revo Egdirb".

Quotes I didn't wake up grumpy this morning. I let her sleep.

XXVII The story about the streets of London being paved with gold originates from the fifteenth century AD when a gold mine was dug in what is now Knightsbridge. The mine still exists. In fact, Harrods was built over it and the upper echelons of the staff there are allowed to go and dig up as much gold as they can carry home every Christmas.

XXVIII Every member of the armed forces in Japan has to learn how to dismantle and put together a Karaoke machine in complete darkness.

XXVIX The original crown jewels were actually made of paste and glass and were worth about seventy-eight pence. However, the ones on show in the Tower of London are, in fact, modern copies made of real gold and jewels and are worth millions. The real crown jewels are in a cardboard box in the attic at Buckingham Palace.

XXX Vampires are real and have been shown to exist by experts. In fact there is a very good chance you have met one, as they all work for either the tax office or the V.A.T.

Quotes *Success means never having to admit that you're unhappy. (Robert Evans)*

XXXI Incredible as it may seem, Taiwan was actually made in Hong Kong and is the only country in the world with a parts and labour warranty and it also carries a guarantee that it's water-proof and chewable. All the spare parts for Taiwan are stored in a colossal warehouse on the outskirts of Kowloon.

XXXII The film Jurassic Park is based on secret research carried out by NASA into recombinant DNA and many different kinds of dinosaurs have been cloned. Lots of fascinating things have been discovered from these experiments, not least of which is the fact that all dinosaurs speak with a Scottish accent and are chronic alco-holics, which is why they died out in the first place. They all ended up sad, drunk and broke in a place called Borassic Park. This has led NASA to rename the genus "Winosaurs".

XXXIII Apples are not fruits. They are, in fact, extremely slow moving insects that hang in trees and drop on their prey. The entire course of science could have been changed if Sir Isaac Newton's head hadn't proved too big to swallow.

XXXIV Corn circles are actually caused by the corn sponta-neously fainting when a rumour about bread is circulated rapidly from ear to ear.

XXXV A giant gerbil was admitted into a Los Angeles hospital for emergency surgery to have Richard Gere removed from his rectum.

XXXVI Bungee jumping was invented by an inebriated Australian who fell off a bridge whilst wearing braces.

XXXVII There are plans afoot to abolish National Insurance numbers, driving licences and passports and replace them with a barcode which you will have tattooed on your forehead. People who don't pay their taxes will also have embarrassing "Special Offer" and "Damaged Goods" signs on their heads until they pay.

XXXVIII You're not allowed to live on the King's Road in London unless you're really good looking.

XXXIX When the Jubilee line was built the workmen discovered a race of little creatures living in tunnels down there. The creatures had dark fur and big front teeth and ran around very quickly on four little legs.

XL Atom bombs never really existed, they were just made up as propaganda to frighten the enemy. The bomb they dropped on Hiroshima was actually a second hand submarine stuffed with the gunpowder from fourteen million bangers.

XLI It has been medically proven that girls who perform fellatio regularly will, on average, live fifteen years longer than girls who don't.

Quotes A man who has taken up some of your time recognises no debt yet it is the only debt he can never repay.

Insults, Put Downs, One Liners, Bin Liners and maybe even some Panty Liners

INSULTS

Please don't think for one minute that I'm suggesting you should go around insulting people. If you do, you will soon achieve that state the ancient Chinese used to refer to as lonely and miserable. However, there are times when you might need a snappy put-down or a scathing witticism. Some people seem to spend their lives being as awkward and obstructive as possible and seem to think their raison d'etre is to make everyone's life as miserable as theirs. Of course, we should pity these poor unfortunates who, for some reason or other, usually seem to end up as civil servants, traffic wardens, bailiffs or pot noodle makers. Of course, we should pity them, but not until we've cut them down to size a bit with a few well chosen words.

PUT DOWNS

You're obviously not a beginner, do you bore for England?

Looking at you reminds me of an old saying: "Time's a great healer, but it's a lousy beautician".

"How much was that jacket?"
"Fifty quid."
"That was a good buy…goodbye to fifty quid."
OR (After feeling a lapel): "What a lovely piece of material, you should have it made into a jacket."

Quotes *No man ever listened himself out of a job.*
(Calvin Coolidge)

That shirt looks like something Marks made when Spencer wasn't looking.

He had a face like a bulldog licking mustard off a nettle.

His IQ is about the same as his waist measurement ... and he's not fat.

If you want a word of advice...I think you're overdoing it a bit on the ugly pills.

His eyesight's so bad he has to wear contact lenses to see his glasses.

Not everyone hates him . . . but then not everyone's met him.

You must get hassled a lot by the STYLE POLICE when you wear that outfit.

It's all very well being a fan of Frankenstein, but you don't have to go THAT far.

Didn't anyone ever tell you that if you stop talking your mouth WON'T heal up?

When she was pregnant, was your mother frightened by a Colobus monkey?

I always stand outside when my girlfriend sings. I wouldn't want the neighbours to think I was beating her up.

If someone is in a bad temper and having a go at you just say: "No, I didn't get laid last night either".

She's so ugly you have to insure your mirrors when she comes round.

She looks like that film star with the lovely hair . . . Lassie.

Is that your aftershave or have you farted?

I thought of the perfect birthday present for you, but it'd be so difficult trying to wrap a spine.

They say owners look like their pets. I know I look a bit like my dog. I take it you keep fish, spiders and cattle.

If a woman insists on being called Ms you can always ask "Is that short for miserable?"

I'm sorry, I didn't realize that you were hard of thinking.

(To a constant chatterer): "You must be made of money. Money talks."

or "I can see why you don't wear lipstick: you can't keep your mouth still long enough to put it on."

Quotes

On reviewing a manuscript from an unknown author, Samuel Johnson sent a letter: "Your manuscript is both good and original. But the part that is good is not original, and the part that is original is not good."

There's less to you than meets the eye.

It was a terrible musical. I came out whistling the scenery. The songs might have been better if someone had set them to music.

If someone is telling a bad joke: "Yes, very interesting. I remember hearing a funny version of that once."

What an interesting face. I've never seen teeth with a centre parting before.

If it wasn't for your face, you'd be quite good looking.

You've a good ear for music. It's such a pity the other one makes you sing so out of tune.

I'd love to have a battle of wits with you but it wouldn't be fair because you're unarmed.

(If someone has a bad smoker's cough) Good sense of tumour you've got there.

I bet I know who ironed your shirt . . . nobody.

His flat is the place that put the 'H' in bedsit.

I like a girl with childbearing lips.

He's got a face like the first person in a horror film to see the monster.

He had a personality bypass at birth.

I wouldn't say he lacks personality, but if he was on his own in a room, there wouldn't be anyone there.

She really thinks she's gorgeous. Last week she tried to sue her bathroom mirror for libel.

GOURMET INSULTS

I'm sorry to bother you but I seem to have been given the taste-free version of this meal by mistake.

I hear the cockroaches in here are so big they help with the washing up.

No, I'm not trying to leave without paying. The rats have got hold of my seat and are dragging me off to their lair.

When I asked for my steak rare I meant lightly cooked,

Quotes *Sure, there've been deaths and injuries in boxing, but none of them serious. (Alan Minter)*

not virtually non-existent and antique.

Did the chef put the dirt on this steak or did you drop it all by yourself?

These oysters are bad. It's like sucking someone's bathing suit.

I just did a food test on this cholesterol. Congratulations, it came out completely food free.

I'd like to complain about this cockroach I found on my plate. It tastes better than the lobster.

No I don't want to hear about your vegetarian specials. I want to eat something that used to have a face.

I asked for peas, not forty four rounds of armour piercing shells.

I wonder if you could help me, I can't seem to work out which of these is the serviette and which is the nan bread.

I wonder if you could explain this item on the bill under "service"? I've asked everyone and we're all quite positive that we didn't have any.

I'm sorry to be fussy, but I think this is the same piece of chicken I sent back last week.

I'm sorry, I thought it said "en cocotte" on the menu not "in creosote".

Can I have my usual table near the sick bucket?

Can you have a quick look on the tin and see if this salmon has the surname "Ella"?

Waiter, I wonder if you'd mind putting your thumb in my soup. At least then it might taste of something.

I'm afraid I couldn't finish the mixed grill, it was all bones. But I'd like to take it back for the dog. Do you have a body bag?

Excuse me waiter, do you think you could stand over

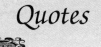

Quotes *Fishing is a delusion entirely surrounded by liars in old clothes. (Don Marquis)*

here and raise your arms? It might keep the flies off my salad.

I noticed a lot of people in the kitchen in white coats. Are they chasing the chef?

When a wine is served at room temperature, it means THIS room, not a sauna in the Sahara.

Waiter, this chicken is very underdone. Will you take it back and have it cooked properly? But bear in mind that any eggs it lays on the way to the kitchen are mine.

Yes, I'm very sorry about the damage to the table, it was careless of me to spill a glass of house wine on the paintwork. If you bring me a radiation suit I'd be more than happy to clear it up.

Your cabaret artist looks desperately ill. Has she been eating here?

I wonder if you could help me, I've just been down-stairs and I can't seem to work out which one of the two rooms is the kitchen and which the toilet.

Waiter, I know it's a little presumptuous of me, but if I give you a large tip would you pop outside . . . and stay there.

The steak was a little over-done. In fact, I'm writing this cheque with it.

I'm sorry, I didn't realize B.B.Q. stood for Badly Burned Quadruped.

Do you think you could send over that male Flamenco dancer with the cuban heels. This steak needs tenderising.

I wanted a jacket potato . . . not a studded leather bike jacket potato.

Is this prawn supposed to be a lobster? Do you think you could bring me a shellfish with a higher calibre shell?

I asked for a deep pan pizza, not a bed pan pizza.

I'm sorry, do you mind if I eat while you smoke?

Quotes *His face was a mask of blood, I think he must have a cut somewhere. (Henry Cooper)*

HOW TO INSULT PEOPLE IN THEIR OWN LANGUAGE

Now that we're in Europe it might be useful to know how to insult people in their native tongue. Here are one or two that might be useful one day:

"GET LOST" IN:

GERMAN . . . Hau'ab
SPANISH . . . A ver si te pierdes de vista!
FRENCH . . . Allez vous faire voir!
ITALIAN . . . Va all'inferno.

"RUBBISH!" IN:

GERMAN . . . Unsinn.
SPANISH . . . Babieca.
FRENCH . . . Foutaise.
ITALIAN . . . Scioccezze.
(Shocketzay)

"MORON" IN:

GERMAN . . . Nackter Wilder.
SPANISH . . . Carcamal.
FRENCH . . . Cretin.
ITALIAN . . . Deficiente.

"BALDY" IN:

GERMAN . . . Geruptftes Huhn.
SPANISH . . . Cateto.
FRENCH . . . Tete d'oeuf.
ITALIAN . . . Testa pelata.

"JOBSWORTH" IN:

GERMAN . . . Bornierter Lackel.
SPANISH . . . Despreciable idiota.
FRENCH . . . Borne.
ITALIAN . . . Idiota meschino.

"BLOCKHEAD" IN:

GERMAN . . . Schwach im Kopf.
SPANISH . . . Majareta.
FRENCH . . . Dingue.
ITALIAN . . . Pazzoide.
(Patzoeeday)

Quotes *A good sport has to lose to prove it.*

LIST OF DESCRIPTIONS OF BLOCKHEADS

He/She's . . .

. . . two sandwiches short of a picnic.

. . . three tracks short of an album.

. . . got a few loose toys in the attic.

. . . a few sticks short of a bundle.

. . . a couple of rashers short of the full breakfast.

. . . not playing with a fully strung racket.

. . . one sock short of a pair.

. . . three balloons short of a party.

. . . eight draws off a pools win.

. . . a few trees short of a forest.

. . . two eggs short of an omelette.

. . . not playing with a full deck.

. . . a couple of shrubs short of an herbaceous border.

. . . not quite the full shilling.

. . . a couple of spanners short of a toolkit.

. . . two dice short of a crap game.

. . . two poppadoms short of a curry.

. . . hasn't got both oars in the water.

. . . four claws short of a paw.

. . . a couple of cans short of a six-pack.

Basically, the lift doesn't go all the way to the top.

IF SOMEONE'S DRUNK

He / She's

. . . disappearing off the radar.

. . . losing it on the corner.

. . . got to keep his head back so he doesn't spill any.

. . . got his comedy legs on tonight.

. . . at the pint of no return.

. . . one drink off two too many.

Quotes   Skiing combines outdoor fun with knocking down trees with your face. (Dave Barry)

Things That Make You Go Hmm...
(Some guidelines for life)

Don't marry someone until you've seen them with a bad head cold.

To avoid parking fines: Remove the windscreen wipers from your car.

You can never lose an intellectual argument if you have a kipper and your opponent has an exhaust pipe.

Why didn't Noah swot the flies?

Why worry about tomorrow when today is so far off?

If you win the Tour de France, think twice before doing a lap of honour.

Don't let life knock all the life out of you.

A prune is just a very experienced plum.

It's better to be lucky than good.

People deserve what they settle for.

There's no such thing as bad weather, only inadequate clothing.

Early to bed, early to rise, makes a man knackered, grouchy and generally no fun to be with.

There is no other name for Thesaurus.

Famous people are just nonentities that everybody knows about.

Make your MP work . . . Don't re-elect him.

An elephant is just a flea with an ego.

The best time to run away is BEFORE you're dead.

If a film is not worth missing, should you go?

A wise man goes to the toilet when he can. A fool goes when he has to.

If your enemy wrongs you, buy each of his children a drum. (Chinese proverb)

Recycled paper parachutes might be cheap, but they're no bargain.

Don't covet thy neighbour's ass. He might give you the damned thing.

If you're thinking about early retirement, spend an afternoon watching daytime TV.

What should the person with everything do with the Crab Nebula?

Diplomacy is the art of letting someone else have your way.

Quotes *That's cricket Harry, you get that sort of thing in boxing. (Frank Bruno)*

Don't have your waste disposal unit fixed by a man called Lefty.

The person who spends his days doing unnecessary things will have an unnecessary life.

Never play cards with a man called Doc.

When talking to an idiot make sure he's not doing the same.

To the leaden heart the sun is but a caster of shadows (K. Ghibran)

People in glass houses should sack their architect.

Many a true word is spoken in Chester.

No wife ever killed her husband while he was washing up.

If something's worth doing . . . it's worth paying someone to do it properly.

The jewels are irrelevant. It's what's UNDER the crown that matters.

Still waters run deep, but fizzy ones taste better.

Whatever you tell them, people always make tea or coffee the way THEY like it.

Never put off until tomorrow what you can forget forever today.

Laugh and the World laughs with you. Cry and you probably have a better grasp of the situation.

Don't bungee jump unless you have plenty of elastic.

Cats are people too, they're just not very bright people.

"You haven't got the guts to pull that trigger" is almost always a bad thing to say.

You wouldn't buy a car that needs "A lot of attention" so why go out with someone with the same problem.

Nobody ever got rich by doing sit-ups.

When crossing the road remember: better safe than lorry.

Quotes *My mum says I used to fight my way out of the cot, but I can't remember. That was before my time.* (*Frank Bruno*)

A cat may look at a King, but I'll lay odds it doesn't understand even the basic principals of monarchy.

Going to sleep while driving is bad, but waking up driving can be worse.

You can stop almost anything from functioning by hitting it with a large rock. (Bell's third law)

Once the map of your life unfolds, it's very difficult to re-fold it. Especially in wind.

Unfortunately, history is against the meek inheriting the Earth.

The man who turns the other cheek is probably picking up a baseball bat.

Even the World's most beautiful people have belly-button fluff.

In the land of the blind the one-eyed man can play some brilliant practical jokes.

If you take a sideways look at lateral thinking it's just like real life.

Always offer to pay for junk food with junk money.

A laugh is just a smile that bursts all over your face.

Irony: make-up tested on animals to make humans look less like beasts.

Four things never come back: the spoken word; the speeding arrow; the past and crushed velvet loon pants.

People will believe anything if you whisper it.

The things that come to those that wait are probably not worth waiting for.

The rich old man who invited the gorgeous young girl up to his room to help him write his Will wasn't stupid.

Man cannot live by cred alone.

If you see a space man . . . park in it man.

Remember, whatever the weather's like . . . it's better than nothing.

Quotes

England were beaten in the sense that they lost. (Dickie Davis)

People never forget a favour . . . if they did it.

Why don't people who believe in reincarnation leave all their money to themselves?

If you ask for some wine with a little body, don't be surprised to find a dead fly in it.

A secret is either not worth keeping or too good to keep.

If blondes have more fun, we need to invent a word for what blonde twins in suspenders have.

If you stretch the truth too far people will be able to see through it.

It's better to be homesick than heresick.

Idiot proof systems are no match for system proof idiots.

Every man is allowed sixteen wives: four better, four worse, four richer and four poorer.

If you don't take care of your body, where will you live?

Big men have painful knuckles.

A man with a watch will always know the time. A man with two watches is never sure.

Quotes The nice thing about being a celebrity is that if you bore people they think it's their fault. (Henry Kissinger)

The Worst Jokes in this Book

It's always good to have a few naff jokes up your sleeve. They're especially useful when the conversation starts heading towards politics or the existence of God from which it may never return.

I'm not for one minute claiming to have written these jokes. They are merely gags I've heard over the years that made me laugh so I'm passing them on in the hope that you might find them funny too. It might help if your audience is drunk when you tell them.

1 When a streaker ran past the convent the Mother Superior had a stroke . . . but the others weren't fast enough.

2 Two guys were looking at some shirts in a shop window. One said "That's the one I'd get" and a cyclops came round the corner and kicked his head in.

3 A bloke is wandering through town when he notices a lecture on the Paranormal at the Town Hall so he goes in and sits down. The lecturer asks the audience if any of them have ever had any strange experiences with ghosts. Our friend puts his hand up and says, "I have."
"What kind of experience was it?" asks the lecturer.
"Well," says our friend, blushing, "It was a sexual experience."
The lecturer is amazed "You had a sexual experience with a ghost?"
"Oh, sorry," says the man. "I thought you said a goat."

4 A guy checks into an hotel and is instantly smitten by the receptionist. He sees her in the bar later on and begins to chat her up. She tells him from the outset that she is a religious girl and not interested in any hanky panky but he points out that "The Bible says it's OK" and eventually she ends up in his room. The man tries to kiss her and she refuses until he points out that "The Bible says it's OK." Finally he goes for the big one but she says "Hang on, show me in the Bible where it says THIS is OK." The guy picks up the Bible from the hotel dressing table and turns to the fly-leaf where someone had written: "The receptionist's an easy lay."

5 Two married couples go on holiday together. One night, after a few drinks, they decide to make things a little more exciting by changing partners. The next morning the two husbands were chatting at the breakfast table. "Well," said one. "I must admit I rather enjoyed last night." "Me too," said the other. "I wonder how the girls got on?"

6 Girl to boyfriend in her parents' lounge, "Sometimes my father takes things apart to see why they don't go." Boy: "Yeah, so what?" Girl: "So you'd better go."

7 Q. Why does the Mersey run through Liverpool?
A. If it walked it'd get mugged.

8 Two drunks get on a train home. They are both clutching a bottle and a sausage roll. The first drunk unwraps his sausage roll and takes a bite as the train enters a tunnel. "Have you eaten your sausage roll yet?" he asks his friend. "No," his friend replies. "Well don't," the man exclaims, "I took a bite out of mine and went blind."

9 A man goes into a shoe shop, and points out a pair of shoes to the assistant. The assistant sizes him up and says, "Would that be a size ten, sir?" "No, make it a size eight," replies the man. "With all due respect, sir, you look more like a ten to me," says the assistant. "Yes I am," says the man. "But I want size

Quotes *Drink not to my past, which is weak and indefensible,*
Nor to my present, which is not above reproach;
But let us drink to our futures, which, thank God, are
immaculate. (Leone P. Forkner)

eight. You see my wife has left me, my business has gone bankrupt, my thirteen year old daughter is pregnant and my son's in jail and the only pleasure I'm going to get out of life is going home and taking these bloody shoes off."

10 A young guy goes back to his girlfriend's house for the first time. They sneak in quietly, but soon after they begin cuddling on the settee the boy says, "I've got to go to the loo." "You can't use the toilet," she says. "It's right next door to my parents' bedroom and they'll hear you. You'll have to move the dishes in the kitchen sink aside and go there." The boy disappears into the kitchen and a few minutes later calls to the girl in an urgent whisper: "Have you got any paper?"

Quotes *A good answer knows when to stop.*

11 Jeremy Beadle and Lloyd Grossman were crossing the road when they were hit by a large truck with rusty spikes on the front. They went to Hell and suffered an eternity of agony and degradation. This isn't really a joke . . . I just thought I'd cheer you up a bit.

12 Q: What's grey, sits at the end of the bed and takes the piss out of you? A: A kidney dialysis machine.

13 Hymie Steinberg passed away suddenly. His wife, Golda, dutifully made all the arrangements and went down to the local paper to put an announcement in the births, marriages and deaths section. "I don't want to spend a fortune. Just put 'Hymie's dead'." "But madam," replied the editor. "Our minimum price for an entry is for six words, so you may as well use them." "Very well," said Golda. "In that case put 'Hymie's dead. Volvo estate for sale.'"

14 A young man is standing in the kitchen at a fairly boring party when the most gorgeous girl he has ever seen walks in. He asks her if she would like a drink but she says she doesn't drink. Then he offers her a cigarette but she declines, saying she doesn't smoke. He asks her what she does and discovers she's an heiress and spends all her time jetting around the World with friends. Finally, he asks if he can see her home and she says yes. When they arrive he is stunned at the magnificent house and can't resist saying: "I have to tell you you're the most wonderful girl I've ever met. You don't smoke or drink, you're beautiful, intelligent and witty and incredibly rich." "Yes," she says. "I'm also incredibly horny, would you like to come inside?" She opens the door and right in the middle of the entrance hall is a pile of broken glass, a dung heap and a dismembered horse. "Christ!" he says. "What's all that?" "Well," says the girl. "I didn't say I was tidy, did I?"

15 a young man had an unfortunate accident and

Quotes *It's not easy to get a snooker when there's only one ball on the table. (Ted Lowe)*

lost an eye. At the hospital he was shown a book of replacement eyes so he could choose one. He picked a superbly crafted glass eye out, but when he heard the price he realized he would never be able to afford it. In fact, after looking at the prices of all the reasonable looking eyes, he realized that the only one he could afford was a rather unconvincing affair made of plywood so he plumped for this one. He was very self-conscious about his cheap wooden eye and tended to stay at home a lot wearing sunglasses. However, one night he thought to himself: "This is no way for a young man with at least one good eye to behave" and he decided to go out and have a good time. He dressed up and went to an nearby night club. He sat in a corner for a while, still nervous about approaching any of the gorgeous women there in case they made fun of his eye. Just as he was worrying about this he noticed a girl with a hump on her back sitting alone at the far end of the club. "She might not

mind dancing with someone with a plywood eye," he thought, so he wandered over, smiling and said "Excuse me but would you like to dance?" The girl had never been asked before and was excited. She looked into his face and said "Would I!" and the young man said "Oh sod off then, you bloody old hunch-back."

16 A man is in a shop with his tight fisted mate. Suddenly two gunmen burst in and demand everyone's money. While the first raider is searching everyone the man's friend nudges him saying, "Here take this." "Don't give me a gun," says the man. "I don't want to be a hero." "It's not a gun," says his friend. "It's the ten quid I owe you."

17 Q: What do you call a three foot high Jamaican?
A: A yardie.

18 A man decides to go fishing. He takes his rod, cuts a hole in the ice and sits down on his little fold up chair for a good "fish". After

Quotes *The wicket didn't do too much, but when it did, it did too much. (Mike Gatting)*

a couple of minutes he hears a booming voice say "THERE ARE NO FISH UNDER THE ICE." He looks all around but can see no-one so he just puts it down to overwork and continues fishing. The voice booms out again with an even more commanding tone "THERE ARE NO FISH UNDER THE ICE." The man looks up and says nervously "Is that you God?" The voice booms out once more "NO, IT'S THE MANAGER OF THE ICE-RINK."

Quotes Hollywood is a place where people from Iowa mistake each other for stars. (Fred Allen)

Stunning Facts to Boggle the Mind *continued*

6

On the death of his mother's cousin, Queen Elizabeth, James the sixth of Scotland became King of England. Certain people at court, however, thought that he might be taking favouritism a little far when he granted the lands of Canada to his friend The Earl of Stirling, for a rent of one penny per annum.

7

Henry VIII was very fond of gambling but was regularly short of the requisite funds to pay his gambling debts. However, for a King this isn't always a problem: on one occasion he bet the bells of St. Paul's Cathedral . . . and lost.

8

A well-loved missionary called Herr Schwartz died in Delhi. At his funeral, as per his last wishes, his favourite hymn was sung. The assemblage, though, were somewhat taken aback when Herr Schwartz began singing along from inside his coffin. It seems that the diagnosis of death had been less than accurate and he came to just in time.

9

A Mr Rodique caused quite a stir when he left his flat in Hamden, Connecticut. The new tenants were rather upset when they found a pair of neatly dissected human arms under the sink. Mr Rodique was an orthopaedic surgeon who had taken the arms from Yale School of Medicine to practice on at home. Whilst packing he had simply forgotten all about them.

10

The human body is indeed a wonderful thing. It contains enough iron to make a spike capable of supporting the body, enough fat for seven bars of soap, enough carbon to fill 9,000 pencils and enough phosphorous for the heads of 2,000 matches.

11

A New York artist decided he had had enough and threw himself off the Empire State Building from an 86th floor window. However, a freak gust of wind caught him and blew him through the window of NBC television on the 83rd floor where there was a live show in progress. Not wanting to miss an opportunity, the artist was interviewed and

admitted that as soon as he'd jumped he'd regretted it.

12

In 1959 an American farmer named Arthur Robby announced that eating fish was sacriligious as he was convinced that Christ would shortly be returning to Earth in the guise of a mackerel.

13

In 1954, a Mr Harry Mills purchased a public telephone box and installed it in his London flat so that he didn't disturb his neighbours while he perfected his version of "Onward Christian Soldiers" played on two mouth-organs.

14

In 1969 the dockers at the port of Darwin, Australia, demanded extra pay for unloading a shipment of toilet fixtures . . . because they were embarrassed.

16

There is a mysterious night prowler in the town of Devonport with the strange habit of hurling unopened packets of Co-ops best

Quotes *I've read a book every night for the last twelve years. I've only got two chapters to go.*

bangers into people's gardens.

17

The national flag of Italy was designed by Napoleon Bonaparte.

18

In 1972, 4,787,092 vehicles went from Kent to Essex, through the Dartford Tunnel, but only 4,761,321 came back. No-one seems to know where the odd 25,000 or so cars went.

19

Every day, the streets of London are treated to a deluge of a million pints of dogs' urine and seventy tons of excrement. Not exactly what you might call "Paved with gold."

20

Since the Eiffel Tower was built in 1889, four people per year have jumped off it.

21

When peeling potatoes, men use up 2.7 calories of energy but women only use 1.29. We must be doing something wrong.

22

In one year, 3,647 Americans with one thing in common were sacked. One fifth were fired for drug abuse and the rest for alcoholism, mental illness and disciplinary problems. The common factor . . . they all had access to nuclear weapons.

23

According to medical experts, it is possible for a man with a healthy liver to drink half a pint of beer an hour, indefinitely, without getting drunk. Honestly, your Honour.

24

Tarantulas can survive for two and a half years without food. However, I wouldn't want to be around when they get hungry again.

25

The manufacturers of "Monopoly" print more money each year than the U.S. treasury.

Quotes *The poor wish to be rich, the rich wish to be happy, the single wish to be married, and the married wish to be dead. (Ann Landers)*

THIS HAS NOTHING TO DO WITH THE BOOK, WE'VE JUST ALWAYS FANCIED DRESSING UP LIKE THIS.